German Meals at Oma's

TRADITIONAL DISHES
for THE HOME COOK

Gerhild Fulson

FOUNDER OF
Just like Oma

PAGE STREET
PUBLISHING CO.

PAGE STREET
PUBLISHING CO.

Copyright © 2018 Gerhild Fulson

First published in 2018 by
Page Street Publishing Co.
27 Congress Street, Suite 105
Salem, MA 01970
www.pagestreetpublishing.com

Distributed by Macmillan, sales in Canada by The Canadian Manda Group.

22 21 20 19 18   1 2 3 4 5

ISBN-13: 978-1-62414-623-7
ISBN-10: 1-62414-623-6

Library of Congress Control Number: 2018951647

Cover and book design by Meg Baskis for Page Street Publishing Co.
Photography by Toni Zernik
Food styling by Scott Wiese

Printed and bound in the United States

So whether you eat or drink, or whatever you do, do it all for the glory of God.

—1 CORINTHIANS 10:31 (NLT)

Contents

Introduction

I'm often asked what Germany's most beloved traditional dish is. That one dish that most reflects our culture. My answer: there isn't just one. Deutschland has such a fusion of tantalizing, hearty cuisines, that it's hard to choose. Touring throughout the country is a delicious adventure, filled with tastes that rekindle precious memories of my *mutti*'s (mom's) Sunday dinners.

My parents immigrated to Canada when I was still a toddler. Mutti loved to cook and Papa loved to bake. However, it wasn't easy for them. In the 1950s, it was almost impossible to find the ingredients needed to make the traditional meals they so craved. However, their creativity and inventiveness won out. Together, they imparted to me a love for German foods.

To help my sisters and me, Mutti typed out her old handwritten German recipes in English and added lots of handwritten notes in English. I'm so glad she did, and Thüringer Klösse (Potato Dumplings from Raw Potatoes; page 187), Rouladen (Beef Rolls; page 180) and Apfel-Rotkohl (Red Cabbage with Apples; page 184) are still my favorites. Of course, Kartoffelsalat mit Mayo (Potato Salad with Mayo; page 105), Sauerbraten (Marinated Braised Beef; page 22) and Falscher Hase (Meatloaf; page 102) are not far behind!

My first trip back to Germany happened in 2006, when my hubby and I journeyed throughout our birth country for five weeks. Taking a bus tour that went through all the regions was a wonderful adventure, and we've returned almost every year since.

Being able to go back to Germany regularly on behalf of the ministry we are involved in is such a blessing. Combining our love for photography with the excitement of searching out local eateries makes these trips wunderbar. Whether it's sloshing barefoot over the tidal flats in Schleswig-Holstein's Wadden Sea to reach a *hallig* (a type of small island) for lunch before the tide turns or roaming through Neuschwanstein Castle in Bavaria and finding the best potato salad at a nearby *wirtshaus* (restaurant), these are memories that will stay with us forever.

Coming home and trying to re-create these meals was sometimes a real challenge. That's when I recalled what Mutti taught me and I got creative and inventive. Being busy, just like most *omas* (grandmothers), I've found that many times there are other ways to get the same or similar delicious results. Sometimes the method changes. Other times, the necessity to use local ingredients influences the final dish.

Do these meals taste exactly like the original, traditional ones? No, not always. Sometimes it's impossible to make them just like they are made in Germany. It's difficult to find the right kind of potato, the right type of flour, the right kind of bacon, the list goes on. However, if you are willing to compromise a bit, you can still enjoy a "German" meal wherever in the world you call home.

Oma's Ecke

Throughout the book, you'll find *Oma's Ecke* (Grandma's Corner) where I share extra tips and tricks that are useful—not just for that recipe, but throughout your cooking journey. Sometimes it's something my *mutti* taught me. Sometimes it's something I found out the hard way. Sometimes it's something that happened accidentally to make the meal extraordinary.

For example, I like to use clarified butter when I fry foods. In Germany, you can buy *butterschmalz* (clarified butter). Not so, over here in North America. Ghee is available nowadays, and it is very similar, but it has a nutty flavor. I found out quite by accident that I can easily make my own *butterschmalz* in my slow cooker.

A pound of unsalted butter, on low heat with the lid slightly ajar, after two hours in your slow cooker, will be ready to be used for frying. Just remove the top "scum" layer and slowly pour that liquid gold through a cheesecloth-lined sieve into a mason jar. Be careful not to stir up the milk solids that have settled on the bottom. That liquid gold, the *butterschmalz*, has a higher burning point than regular butter. It's perfect for frying your schnitzel (page 118 and page 138), your onions and anything else your heart fancies. It will keep for weeks, if it lasts that long.

Join me as we take a culinary trip to all the *bundesländer* (states) and see what traditional classics Oma would prepare for you if you visited her there! Then go and make these meals as a treasure to pass on to your own family, just like my *mutti* did.

Gerhild Fulson

Berlin

Germany's capital and largest city, Berlin, is also one of the country's smallest states. Small, perhaps, but filled with hundreds of parks, gardens, palaces, museums and art galleries to roam through. Enjoy the river cruises, take a guided bike tour, look down from a hot-air balloon and shop your way through the malls and down the famous boulevard, Kurfürstendamm.

Visit during one of the festivals, perhaps during *Berlinale* (the second largest film festival in the world) or during Advent (with more than twenty Christmas markets to choose from). Culinary treats from around the world are available in the countless restaurants and *imbisse* (snack bars) and, of course, at your *oma's* house!

Though filled with international visitors and immigrants who have influenced the culture and local eateries, traditional Berliner recipes are still plentiful. These are the typical foods I grew up with, made just like my *mutti* made them.

Königsberger Klopse

(KÖNIGSBERG MEATBALLS IN CAPER SAUCE)

In a recent German poll, this dish was considered one of the most popular regional dishes throughout the whole country. With a history that goes back to the Prussian city of Königsberg, the recipe for these meatballs has changed little over time. No wonder, since they are melt-in-your-mouth delicious and their creamy sauce is an explosion of flavors with hints of lemon and capers. These *Königsberger Klopse*, considered a true Berliner dish, are usually served with boiled or mashed potatoes and pickled beets.

4½ tbsp (67 g) butter, divided

2 small shallots, finely diced

2 tbsp (5 g) finely chopped fresh parsley

1 stale kaiser roll, sliced

1 cup (250 ml) lukewarm water

4 tbsp (32 g) all-purpose flour

4 cups (1 L) hot chicken or beef broth

1 dried bay leaf

¾ tsp salt, plus more as needed

¼ tsp freshly ground black pepper, plus more as needed

1½ lb (680 g) lean ground beef or beef and pork mix

1 large egg

1 tbsp (15 g) German mustard (see *Oma's Ecke*)

¼ tsp paprika

3 finely diced anchovies, optional

1 to 2 tbsp (15 to 30 ml) fresh lemon juice

2 tbsp (17 g) capers, with a bit of their juice

½ cup (115 g) sour cream

Pinch of sugar and freshly grated nutmeg

In a small skillet over medium-high heat, melt ½ tablespoon (7 g) of the butter. Add the shallots and sauté until they have softened, about 2 minutes. Add the parsley and sauté for 1 minute. Set the skillet aside to cool.

Place the kaiser roll in a small bowl. Add the water and let the roll soak until it's needed.

Make the sauce by melting the remaining 4 tablespoons (60 g) of butter in a medium saucepan over medium heat. Whisk in the flour until the roux is smooth, which will take about 1 minute, but do not let it brown. Gradually whisk in the hot broth, stirring until the sauce is smooth. Add the bay leaf, cover the saucepan and simmer the sauce for 5 minutes. Season with salt and pepper as needed, and keep the sauce warm.

To make the meatballs, squeeze the kaiser roll in your hands to remove the water and crumble it into a large bowl. Add the beef, egg, mustard, the remaining ¾ teaspoon of salt, the remaining ¼ teaspoon of pepper, paprika, cooled shallot mixture and anchovies (if using). Mix well using your hands. Form the mixture into 1½-inch (3.8-cm) balls.

Add the meatballs to the sauce, increase the heat to medium and bring the sauce to a simmer. Reduce the heat to low and cover the saucepan. Let the sauce gently simmer for 15 minutes, carefully stirring occasionally to make sure nothing sticks to the bottom.

Remove the saucepan from the heat and, using a slotted spoon, transfer the meatballs to a serving bowl and cover it to keep the meatballs warm. Remove the bay leaf from the sauce and stir in the lemon juice, capers and sour cream. Season the sauce with the sugar and nutmeg and additional salt and pepper. Pour the sauce over the meatballs and serve.

What if you can't find German mustard? Then just use your favorite one. For this recipe, a brown one is good, but yellow mustard works as well.

Eisbein mit Sauerkraut

(PORK HOCKS WITH SAUERKRAUT)

In southern Germany, pork hocks, or knuckles, are served roasted with a crispy skin. In Berlin, however, the hocks are boiled, and the meat is served on a bed of sauerkraut. The same cut of meat, but with two totally different flavors. The Berliner one has a juicier and more tender meat hidden beneath the fat and rind that normally are not eaten. However, I do recall seeing my *opa* (grandfather) eat that fat layer covered with hot German mustard!

Eisbein translates to "ice leg" and appears to refer to an interesting use for these knuckle bones many, many years ago. Their shape and strength allowed them to be strapped to shoes, turning them into skates to use on the frozen ponds. Today, when it is freezing out, Berliner pork hocks are the perfect hearty, cold-weather dish, often served with boiled potatoes and pureed peas. And yes, don't forget that mustard.

PORK HOCKS

Water, as needed

2 medium onions, quartered

1 small leek, coarsely chopped

1 cup (227 g) cubed celeriac or 1 cup (100 g) coarsely chopped celery

1 large carrot, coarsely chopped

1 dried bay leaf

2 cloves

1 tsp black peppercorns

1 tsp salt

2.2 lbs (1 kg) fresh, meaty pork hocks

SAUERKRAUT

1 tbsp (15 g) butter

¾ cup (115 g) diced onion

1 large Cortland or Granny Smith apple, peeled and diced

2 cups (284 g) sauerkraut, well drained

1 cup (250 ml) pork hocks cooking broth

1 tsp caraway seeds

1 dried bay leaf

Salt and freshly ground black pepper, as needed

To cook the pork hocks, fill a kettle with water, bring it to a boil and keep it hot until needed.

Place the onions, leek, celeriac, carrot, bay leaf, cloves, peppercorns and salt in a deep saucepan large enough to hold the pork hocks. Add water until the saucepan is half full and bring the water to a boil over high heat.

Add the pork hocks, adding the boiling water from the kettle if needed so that the meat is totally submerged. Reduce the heat to medium-low and simmer for 2 to 2½ hours, or until the meat can be easily separated from the bone.

Start the sauerkraut about 1 hour before the meat is finished cooking. In a medium saucepan, melt the butter over medium heat. Add the onion and sauté until it is translucent, about 5 minutes. Mix in the apple, sauerkraut, cooking broth, caraway seeds and bay leaf. Reduce the heat to medium-low and bring the mixture to a simmer. Cover the saucepan and cook for 30 minutes, checking frequently to make sure there is enough liquid and adding more cooking broth, if needed. Remove the bay leaf. Season the sauerkraut with the salt and pepper.

Remove the hocks from the broth. Either serve the whole hocks with the sauerkraut on the side or separate the meat from the bones and fat. Place the chunks of meat on top of the sauerkraut. Serve with your favorite mustard.

Oma's Ecke

The leftover broth is wonderful to use as a base for a soup. Once refrigerated, remove any fat that hardens on the top. Portion the broth into containers and freeze until needed.

Hoppel Poppel

(POTATO AND EGG HASH)

I grew up with this quick meal, thinking it was just my *mutti*'s way of using leftovers. I never realized this was a traditional Berliner omelet, very similar to the *bauernfrühstück* (farmer's breakfast) served throughout Germany. The actual name for it, *Hoppel Poppel*, has no translation. It's just a fun name for a delicious dish.

Sometimes when making this, I'll omit the eggs if there's leftover gravy from the night before. I pour the gravy over the fried potatoes to heat it through and garnish with the parsley. This always ends up as a special meal, one that can't be replicated exactly, because it really depends on what the leftovers came from. Beef gravy, pork gravy or chicken gravy—they all work. Toss in leftover veggies as well, and you have your own traditional *Hoppel Poppel* (with or without the eggs).

1½ lbs (680 g) Yukon gold potatoes, boiled in their skins, peeled and refrigerated (see *Oma's Ecke*)

1 lb (454 g) cooked meat (ham, beef, chicken, salami and so on)

4 tbsp (60 g) butter, divided

1 cup (150 g) diced onion

6 to 8 large eggs, beaten

Salt and freshly ground black pepper, as needed

2 tbsp (5 g) finely chopped fresh parsley, for garnish

Cut the potatoes into ¼-inch (6-mm) slices. Cut the meat into thin slices or ½-inch (13-mm) cubes.

Melt 2 tablespoons (30 g) of the butter in a large skillet over medium-high heat. Add the potatoes and fry until lightly browned, 5 to 10 minutes, using a spatula to flip them as they cook.

Push some of the potatoes to the side and add the remaining 2 tablespoons (30 g) of butter and the onion to the clear portion of the skillet. Cook for 3 to 5 minutes, or until the onion is translucent. Mix the onion with the potatoes and add the meat. Fry and flip the mixture occasionally for 2 to 3 minutes, until the potatoes are browned and the meat is warmed through.

Pour the eggs over the potato mixture. After 1 minute, stir gently and continue frying until the eggs have cooked through, 2 to 3 minutes. Season the hash with salt and pepper.

Garnish the hash with the parsley and serve. German pickles are often included on the side.

Oma's Ecke

Ideally, it's a good idea to cook extra potatoes the day before in order to have them ready. But, if you really want this and don't have precooked ones, you can use raw peeled potatoes. Slice them about ¼ inch (6 mm) thick and fry them in the butter, flipping them frequently so they don't stick to the skillet. They'll take at least 10 minutes to cook through. Continue with the recipe as directed.

I use raw potatoes for this when we're camping, frying diced bacon before adding the potatoes. I cook this over an open campfire and the fragrance of the onions and bacon wafting through the campground brings the neighbors by. Just thinking about this makes my mouth water.

Senfeier mit Kartoffeln

(MUSTARD EGGS WITH POTATOES)

When time and money are limited, making a dinner using ingredients that you probably already have in your pantry and fridge is a blessing. When that dinner also tastes good, it's a double blessing. This dinner is one of those. Simply put, it's hard-boiled eggs in a mustard sauce served with potatoes. A crispy green salad is a really nice accompaniment to this. Easy and quick. What's more, kids love it.

1½ lbs (680 g) potatoes, peeled and quartered

1 tsp salt, plus more as needed

8 large eggs

4 tbsp (60 g) butter

4 tbsp (32 g) flour

2½ cups (600 ml) hot vegetable broth (see *Oma's Ecke*)

½ cup (120 ml) heavy cream or milk

3 tbsp (45 g) mustard (see *Oma's Ecke*)

Freshly ground white pepper, as needed

Freshly grated nutmeg, as needed

1 tbsp (15 ml) lemon juice (see *Oma's Ecke*)

Pinch of sugar

2 tbsp (5 g) finely chopped fresh parsley or chives, for garnish

Put the potatoes into a medium saucepan, cover them with water, add the 1 teaspoon of salt and bring the potatoes to a boil over high heat. Cover the saucepan, reduce the heat to medium and simmer until the potatoes are tender, about 20 minutes. Drain the potatoes but leave them in the saucepan. Cover the saucepan with a clean tea towel (to absorb the steam) and cover the tea towel with a lid to keep the potatoes warm.

Meanwhile, in a medium pot, cover the eggs with water and bring the water to a boil over high heat. Boil the eggs for 6 to 8 minutes, drain, rinse under cold water and peel them. Set the eggs aside.

While the potatoes and eggs are cooking, make the sauce by melting the butter in a large skillet over medium heat. Whisk in the flour until the roux is smooth, which will take about 1 minute, but do not let it brown. Gradually whisk in the hot broth and cream, stirring until the sauce is smooth. Reduce the heat to medium-low and simmer for 5 minutes, stirring occasionally. Stir in the mustard and season with additional salt and white pepper, nutmeg, lemon juice and sugar.

Cut the hard-boiled eggs in half. Place them in the sauce, with their cut sides up, to reheat for a few minutes. Divide the potatoes among the dinner plates, spoon the sauce beside them and arrange the egg halves on the sauce. Garnish with the parsley.

Oma's Ecke

This recipe is easy to alter according to your tastes and whatever is in your kitchen. Instead of using vegetable broth, use all milk, chicken stock or even water. Use more liquid if you want a thinner sauce. A spicy mustard is great, and prepared brown mustard (as shown here) and Dijon work well, as does traditional German whole-grain mustard. Try altering the amount of lemon juice you use. Start with a small amount and work your way up until the sauce has the tartness you like.

Leber mit Zwiebeln und Äpfel

(LIVER WITH ONIONS AND APPLES)

I never understood people's dislike for liver. Perhaps it's the bacon, apples and onions that my *mutti* added that made it so good. It's the way she always made it for us, and it's the only way I make it to this day. Known as *Berliner Leber* (Berlin liver), this dish is popular throughout Germany.

4 tbsp (60 g) butter, divided, plus more as needed

8 slices bacon

2 large onions, sliced into ¼-inch (6-mm) rings

3 large Cortland or Granny Smith apples, peeled and cut into ½-inch (13-mm) slices

1 lb (454 g) calf liver, cut into ½-inch (13-mm) slices (see *Oma's Ecke*)

¼ cup (32 g) all-purpose flour

Pinch of ground coriander, optional

Salt and freshly ground black pepper, as needed

Pinch of sugar

In a large skillet over medium heat, melt 1 tablespoon (15 g) of the butter. Add the bacon and fry for about 8 minutes, until it is crispy. Remove the bacon and drain it on a plate lined with a paper towel. Pour the bacon fat into a small bowl, leaving 2 tablespoons (30 ml) in the skillet, and set the bowl aside.

Add the onions to the skillet and sauté for about 10 minutes, until they are caramelized, adding some of the reserved fat, if needed. If the onions start browning too quickly, reduce the heat. Using a slotted spoon, transfer the onions to a medium bowl.

Add the apples to the skillet and sauté for 6 to 7 minutes, or until they are just tender and lightly browned, adding butter if needed. Remove the apples from the skillet and add them to the onions.

Prepare the liver by removing any skin. Put the flour in a flat dish and dredge the liver in it. Add the remaining 3 tablespoons (45 g) of the butter to the skillet over medium heat. Fry the liver for 2 minutes on each side, sprinkling it lightly with the coriander (if using), salt and pepper on each side. Transfer the liver to a serving platter and cover to keep it warm.

Add the onions and apples back to the skillet over medium heat. Stir gently for a few minutes, until they are heated through. Season the onions and apples with salt, pepper and sugar. Place the onions and apples beside the liver. Top with the bacon slices and serve.

Oma's Ecke

If you can't get calf liver, you can use beef, pork or sheep liver. It's advisable to soak those livers in either buttermilk or milk to mellow their strong flavors. If you've a choice which to buy, I highly recommend the calf liver. Yes, it usually is more expensive, but for this recipe, it really is the best.

Mutti often served mashed potatoes and a salad on the side. I like to do the same, although *pommes*, German french fries, are really nice with this as well.

Hamburg

With its international harbor (appropriately called the Gateway to the World), Hamburg has enjoyed access to spices and foreign foods for centuries. Mingling these newcomers with traditional foods has created a truly distinctive cuisine. Yet the old classics are still enjoyed to this day.

These classics can be found when you join the millions that visit the three *volksfeste* (festivals) held annually at *Heiligengeistfeld* (Holy Spirit Field) or on your harbor cruise during *Hafengeburtstag*, a celebration of the "birth" of the harbor in 1189.

With so many places to visit, from the *Miniatur Wunderland* (a miniature wonderland featuring the world's largest model railway) to the platform near the top of St. Michael's Church with views of the port and surrounding countryside, you'll soon be hungry and ready to chow down on some classics of your own.

Sauerbraten

(MARINATED BRAISED BEEF)

Serves 4

This recipe is a wonderful example from my *mutti*'s handwritten cookbook. Served with potato dumplings and red cabbage, it was a meal reserved for special occasions. The meat was always so tender and the gravy was a perfect counterpoint to the red cabbage. What's really awesome is that this is actually quite easy to make. Much of the preparation happens days before you actually cook the meat, making this a great dish for a busy holiday feast.

MARINADE

¾ cup (180 ml) dry red wine

½ cup (125 ml) red wine vinegar

1 cup (250 ml) water

1 medium onion, quartered

2 cloves

6 black peppercorns

2 dried bay leaves

1 tsp salt

ROAST

2 lb (908 g) beef rump, chuck or bottom round roast

Salt and freshly ground black pepper, as needed

3 tbsp (45 g) butter, divided

1 large carrot, thickly sliced

1 medium onion, thickly sliced

1 cup (227 g) cubed celeriac or 1 cup (100 g) coarsely chopped celery

2 cups (500 ml) beef broth or 1 cup (250 ml) beef broth and 1 cup (250 ml) reserved marinade

2 tbsp (19 g) cornstarch mixed with 2 tbsp (30 ml) cold water

½ cup (115 g) sour cream

To make the marinade, pour the wine, vinegar, water, onion, cloves, peppercorns, bay leaves and salt in a medium saucepan. Bring to a boil over high heat. Remove the saucepan from the heat and let the marinade cool.

To make the roast, put the beef in a resealable freezer bag. Pour the cooled marinade over the beef. Seal the bag. Refrigerate the beef for 3 to 5 days, turning it over twice a day.

Remove the beef and strain the marinade into a bowl, reserving it if you will be adding it to the gravy. Dry the beef completely with paper towels and sprinkle it with salt and pepper.

Melt 2 tablespoons (30 g) of the butter in a large saucepan over medium-high heat. Add the beef and brown it well on all sides, about 2 minutes on each side. Transfer the beef to a plate. Add the remaining 1 tablespoon (15 g) of the butter, the carrot, onion and celeriac to the saucepan. Sauté for about 5 minutes, or until the vegetables are slightly softened. Add the broth and the reserved marinade (if using), stirring up the browned bits on the bottom of the saucepan. Transfer the beef back to the saucepan, reduce the heat to low and bring the liquid to a simmer. Cover the saucepan and cook for 2 to 2½ hours, or until the meat is tender.

Transfer the roast to a serving platter and tent it with foil to keep it warm. Either strain the gravy through a sieve and return it to the saucepan or use an immersion blender to create a smooth consistency. Bring the gravy to a boil over medium heat, stirring in just enough cornstarch slurry to thicken it. Simmer for 1 minute and remove from the heat.

In a small bowl, temper the sour cream by stirring several spoonfuls of hot gravy into the sour cream. Stir the sour cream mixture into the gravy. Season the gravy with salt and pepper. Slice the *sauerbraten* and serve with the gravy on the side.

Traditional sides for this dish are Apfel-Rotkohl (Red Cabbage with Apples; page 184) and Schneebällchen (Potato Dumplings from Cooked Potatoes; page 84). Alternatively, Kartoffelpuffer (Potato Pancakes; page 87) and applesauce taste wunderbar with *sauerbraten*.

Frikadellen

(HAMBURG'S HAMBURGERS)

Frikadellen, buletten, fleischklösse, fleischpflanzerl, klopse and *hacksteak* are just some of the names used throughout Germany for a version of what is called the hamburger everywhere else. Though they may look just like regular hamburgers, Hamburg's are deliciously different. Although breadcrumbs can be used as a binding agent along with the egg in a ground meat mixture, the most popular way to do this in Germany is to use stale rolls or bread. Not only is this method a great way to use leftovers, it also gives a lighter texture to the finished meat.

1 stale kaiser roll, sliced

1 cup (250 ml) lukewarm water

5 tbsp (75 g) clarified butter or butter, divided

2 cups (320 g) diced onions

7 oz (200 g) lean ground beef

7 oz (200 g) ground pork

7 oz (200 g) ground veal

2 large eggs

1 tsp salt

½ tsp freshly ground black pepper

4 tbsp (10 g) finely chopped fresh flat-leaf parsley

1 tbsp (15 g) German whole-grain mustard

½ cup (60 g) breadcrumbs, or as needed

Place the kaiser roll in a small bowl. Add the water and let the roll soak until it is needed.

Melt 1 tablespoon (15 g) of the butter in a medium skillet over medium heat. Add the onions and sauté, stirring occasionally, for about 10 minutes, or until they are lightly caramelized. Transfer the onions to a plate to cool and set aside.

In a large bowl, mix together the beef, pork, veal, eggs, salt, pepper, parsley and mustard. Using your hands, squeeze the sliced roll to remove most of the water and crumble it, adding it to the meat mixture. Add the sautéed onions. Mix well, using your hands. If the mixture is too moist and does not hold together, mix in some of the breadcrumbs.

Form the meat mixture into 8 patties about 1 inch (2.5 cm) thick. Put the bread-crumbs on a flat plate. Roll each patty in the crumbs so that all the sides are covered.

In a large skillet, melt the remaining 4 tablespoons (60 g) of butter over medium-high heat. Brown the patties 2 minutes on each side. Turn the heat down to medium-low, cover the skillet and fry the patties for about 8 minutes, turning them occasionally. Reduce the heat if they are browning too quickly. Remove the skillet's lid for the last minute to evaporate the moisture from the crust. The patties' internal temperature should be 160°F (71°C). Transfer the patties to a dish lined with paper towels to drain.

These are delicious when served with potato salad and mustard. Leftovers can be eaten cold the next day.

Do you ever wonder if there's enough seasoning in the raw mixture when you're cooking ground meat? It's easy to check. Simply take a small spoonful of the meat and microwave it for about 20 seconds, or until no pink shows inside. Let the meat cool and taste it. Add more salt and pepper to the meat mixture, if needed. Perhaps some ketchup, mustard or spicy seasoning mix could be added as well. Never again will you have flat-tasting meatballs, meatloaf or hamburgers.

Bratkartoffeln

(FRIED POTATOES)

Serves 4

My *mutti* had three ways to make her fried potatoes. Each was slightly different, but each was absolutely mouthwatering. The first way is the most traditional but needs planning. This is the way most restaurants in Germany make them, because they really are the best. The second way is great if you find yourself with leftover potatoes. The third method is perfect if you're desperate for *bratkartoffeln* and need them now.

Choose your method:

1. Start the day before by cooking the potatoes in their skins in plenty of salted boiling water. They'll take about 20 to 40 minutes, depending on their size. To check if they're tender, poke them with the point of a knife. It should slide in easily. Drain the potatoes, let them cool and peel them. Keep them in the fridge until the next day. (This is considered the best way to make them.)

2. Use leftover boiled potatoes. (See *Oma's Ecke*. This is the quick method.)

3. Use peeled raw potatoes. (These'll take longer to fry and will taste totally different. Different, but delicious.)

2 to 3 tbsp (30 to 45 g) butter, divided

1 cup (150 g) diced onions

8 slices bacon, diced

1¾ lbs (800 g) prepared potatoes (see headnote), cut into ¼-inch (6-mm) slices (see *Oma's Ecke*)

Salt and freshly ground black pepper, as needed

2 tbsp (5 g) finely chopped fresh parsley, for garnish

Melt 1 tablespoon (15 g) of the butter in a large skillet over medium heat. Add the onions and bacon and cook, stirring occasionally, until the fat is rendered and the onions are translucent, 5 to 7 minutes. Using a slotted spoon, transfer the onions and bacon to a medium bowl.

Add the potatoes to the skillet. Fry the potatoes for 5 to 6 minutes, until the bottoms are browned, and gently turn them over. Add the remaining 1 to 2 tablespoons (15 to 30 g) of butter, if needed, to keep them from sticking to the bottom of the skillet. Fry for another 5 to 6 minutes, until most of the potatoes have crispy browned bits on them.

If you are using raw potatoes, cover the skillet with its lid and fry until the potatoes are tender, 10 to 12 minutes. Remove the lid and fry for 5 minutes, turning the potatoes so that most of them have crispy bits.

Add the bacon and onions to the potatoes and season with the salt and pepper, turning the mixture gently to distribute everything. Serve garnished with the parsley.

Oma's Ecke

The best potatoes to use for this are waxy, low-starch ones. All-purpose ones, such as Yukon gold, will also work fine. If you only have starchy ones, use them, but cut them into thicker slices and turn them carefully, so they don't fall apart.

Leftover potatoes are usually *salzkartoffeln* (boiled potatoes) that have been peeled and then boiled in salted water. The first method mentioned in the headnote uses what Germans call *pellkartoffeln* (potatoes boiled in their skins). These are potatoes that are cooked in their skins and then peeled. The texture on the outside of those peeled potatoes is totally different than the leftover boiled ones. That is exactly where the yummy difference in the final product comes from.

Labskaus

(CORNED BEEF HASH)

Once considered a simple dish for sailors and seamen, *labskaus* has become a restaurant staple in Hamburg and other northern German cities. Like many other dishes that have evolved over time, there are so many variations possible. Some things, however, remain constant: the potatoes, the corned beef, the beets and the fried egg. Alter these four ingredients and make this dish your very own. For example, choose whether to make this hash creamy or chunky, mild or spicy, and if you really want to, add that *rollmops* (see *Oma's Ecke*)!

1½ lbs (680 g) peeled Yukon gold potatoes, cubed

1 tsp salt, plus more as needed

3 tbsp (45 g) butter, divided

1 cup (150 g) finely diced onions

1 lb (454 g) canned corned beef, cubed

1 cup (157 g) canned diced red beets, drained and juice reserved

2 tbsp (30 ml) dill pickle brine

2 tbsp (30 ml) reserved beet juice, or more as needed

Freshly ground black pepper, as needed

Freshly grated nutmeg, as needed

4 large eggs (see *Oma's Ecke*)

Fresh parsley, for garnish

1 cup (170 g) canned sliced pickled red beets, drained

2 dill pickles, thickly sliced

Put the potatoes in a medium saucepan, cover them with water, add the 1 teaspoon salt and bring to boil over high heat. Cover the saucepan, reduce the heat to medium-high and simmer until the potatoes are tender, about 15 minutes. Drain, cover and keep them warm.

While the potatoes are cooking, melt 2 tablespoons (30 g) of the butter in a large nonstick skillet over medium heat. Add the onions and sauté for 5 to 7 minutes, or until they are tender but not browned, stirring frequently. Add the corned beef and fry for about 2 minutes, stirring occasionally. Add the diced beets and stir together. Cover the skillet and set it aside until the potatoes are ready.

Mash the potatoes, adding 2 tablespoons (30 ml) of the pickle brine and 2 tablespoons (30 ml) of the beet juice. Add the potatoes to the beef hash, stir well and season with salt, pepper and nutmeg. If the mash is too thick, stir in a bit more beet juice. Cover the saucepan to keep the hash warm.

In a medium skillet over medium heat, melt the remaining 1 tablespoon (15 g) of butter and fry the eggs sunny-side up for 2 to 3 minutes. Arrange the hash on plates, place a fried egg on the side and garnish with the parsley, sliced beets and pickle slices.

Oma's Ecke

If you prefer, you can serve poached eggs instead of fried ones. *Rollmops* (pickled herring fillets) are another traditional garnish for *labskaus*. These fillets can also be finely diced and added to the beef hash as it is cooking.

Verlorene Aalsuppe

(LOST EEL SOUP)

In *Plattdeutsch*, a northern German dialect, this soup has *aal drin*, meaning "everything is in it," which, of course, could include *aal*. However, *aal* means "eel" in German outside the *Plattdeutsch* dialect. So, to keep everyone happy, especially restaurants offering this flavorful soup, *aalsuppe* (eel soup) had to include *aal*. If it didn't, the restaurants could be charged with false advertising, even though their *aal* meant "all" and not "eel." Confused yet? So, the *aal drin suppe* ("everything is in it" soup) without *aal* needed a new name. *Verlorene Aalsuppe*, meaning "lost eel soup," was born. This one has *schwemmklösschen* (swimming dumplings) made from a *brandteig* (choux pastry) dough. The "all" is in it to make it scrumptious. Add eel if you want.

SCHWEMMKLÖSSCHEN DUMPLINGS

½ cup (120 ml) milk

Pinch of salt and freshly grated nutmeg

2 tbsp (30 g) butter

½ cup (65 g) all-purpose flour

1 large egg, beaten

SOUP

5 oz (142 g) dried prunes or dried fruit mix, soaked in water overnight

4 cups (1 L) ham broth made with bouillon or stock cubes (see *Oma's Ecke*)

1½ cups (250 g) diced ham or smoked sausage

3 cups (300 g) fresh or frozen cauliflower florets

1 medium leek, white part only, thinly sliced

1 large rib celery, diced

1 large carrot, diced

Pinch of dried summer savory

1 tbsp (3 g) finely chopped fresh parsley

2 tbsp (30 ml) white wine vinegar

2 tsp (8 g) sugar

Salt and freshly ground black pepper, as needed

Prepare the *schwemmklösschen* by heating the milk, salt, nutmeg and butter in a small saucepan over medium heat until the butter is melted. Bring the mixture to a boil. Remove the saucepan from the heat and add the flour all at once, stirring until the mixture is smooth and comes away from the sides of the saucepan. Return the saucepan to the heat and cook for 1 minute, stirring constantly. Cool for 2 minutes and vigorously stir in the egg until you have a smooth dough. Set aside.

To make the soup, drain the prunes and put them in a large saucepan. Add the broth, ham, cauliflower, leek, celery, carrot and summer savory. Bring to a boil over high heat. Reduce the heat to medium, cover the saucepan and simmer for 15 minutes, or until the vegetables are tender. Add the parsley, vinegar and sugar. Season with the salt and pepper. Keep the soup warm until the dumplings are ready.

Cook the dumplings by bringing a medium saucepan half-full of water to a boil over high heat. Reduce the heat to medium so that the water simmers. Using two water-dipped teaspoons, form small dumplings from the dough and drop them into the simmering water. Cook for 5 to 8 minutes, stirring occasionally to keep the dumplings from sticking, or until they are cooked through.

Serve the soup garnished with the dumplings.

Oma's Ecke

Traditionally, a ham bone is cooked with veggies to get the broth. The veggies are strained out, the broth and the meat are then cooked with new veggies and the dumplings added. If you've a ham bone you want to use, add some coarsely chopped onion, kohlrabi, carrots, celeriac and parsnip to the ham bone. Cover with water. Cook for 1 hour, strain the broth and remove any meat from the bone and continue with the recipe.

Nordrhein-Westfalen

(North Rhine-Westphalia)

The merging of two provinces in 1946 provided an interesting culinary mix. The Westphalians liked hearty foods and the Rhinelanders liked sweet and sour combinations. The result? A wonderful melting pot of flavors. Flavors that'll entice even the pickiest eaters.

Indulging is what you'll do as you travel throughout this state. There are centuries-old historical fairs to visit: the *Rheinkirmes* in Düsseldorf, a fun fair that goes back to 1453; the *Pützchens Markt* in Bonn, with origins in the fourteenth century; or one of the most traditional of all folk festivals, the *Haaner Kirmes,* believed to date back to the ninth century. These fairs are places that mix food with entertainment of all types, and people have savored it for centuries.

Zwiebelfleisch

(BEEF AND ONIONS)

Attend any wedding in Westphalia and you're likely to come across this traditional dish as one of the starter courses. There's no reason to wait for an invitation when this is so easy to make at home and serve as the main meal, with boiled potatoes and a green salad.

MEAT

2 lb (908 g) beef bottom round, sirloin or rump roast (see *Oma's Ecke*)

2 tbsp (30 g) clarified butter or 2 tbsp (30 ml) neutral oil

6 cups (1.5 L) beef broth

1 large leek, coarsely chopped

1 cup (227 g) cubed celeriac or 1 cup (100 g) coarsely chopped celery

1 small bunch fresh parsley

1 medium onion, peeled and quartered

2 dried bay leaves

Water, as needed, optional

GRAVY

3 tbsp (45 g) clarified butter or 3 tbsp (45 ml) neutral oil

1 lb (454 g) onions, thinly sliced

2 tbsp (16 g) all-purpose flour

2 cups (500 ml) reserved strained cooking broth

1 tbsp (15 g) *Düsseldorf* or Dijon mustard

1 tbsp (15 ml) white wine vinegar

Salt and freshly ground black pepper, as needed

Prepare the meat by trimming away any excess fat and removing any silver skin from the beef. Melt the butter in a large, deep saucepan over high heat. Add the beef and brown for about 2 minutes on each side. Add the broth, stirring up any browned bits on the bottom of the saucepan. Add the leek, celeriac, parsley, onion and bay leaves. Add water, if needed, until the roast is submerged. Bring the mixture to a boil, reduce the heat to low, cover the saucepan and simmer gently for 2 to 2½ hours. Transfer the beef to a platter, cover it and set it aside. Strain the broth for use in the gravy and reserve 2 cups (500 ml). Any extra can be saved to make soup.

Make the gravy by melting the butter in a large skillet over medium heat. Add the onions and cook until they are translucent, about 5 minutes. Do not let them brown. Dust the flour over the onions and stir. Slowly add the cooking broth, stirring well to make sure that no lumps form. Bring the mixture to a boil, reduce the heat to low, cover the skillet and simmer for 20 minutes, stirring occasionally. If the gravy becomes too thick, add a bit more broth. Stir in the mustard and vinegar. Season with salt and pepper.

Slice the beef into ½-inch (13-mm) thick slices. Place the slices into the simmering gravy and let the meat warm to serving temperature. Transfer the meat to a plate and serve the gravy on the side.

Oma's Ecke

Boiling beef is a very common cooking method in Germany. There are two ways to ensure tender meat, both of which involve sealing its pores before the actual simmering takes place.

The one method, as used in Tafelspitz mit Meerrettich-Sosse (Boiled Beef with Horseradish Sauce; page 148), plunges the meat into boiling water. That way, the pores are immediately sealed and afterward the meat is very gently simmered until it is tender. It's a quick and easy method.

In this *Zwiebelfleisch* recipe, the meat is first thoroughly seared on all sides before the broth and water are added and brought to a simmer. In this method, a richer flavor is developed, yet it takes a bit more work and time. I think you'll agree that it's worth it!

Dicke Bohnen und Speck

(BROAD BEANS AND BACON)

Broad beans, also known as fava beans, are commonly used in Nordrhein-Westfalen and throughout northern Germany with the city of Erfurt using these beans, which it calls *pufferbohnen* (broad beans), as its town mascot! But instead of parading around dressed as a bean, here *dicke bohnen* are enjoyed with bacon in a creamy sauce. A traditional accompaniment for this are *mettwürstchen* (smoked pork sausages) and potatoes, either boiled or mashed, that have been seasoned with freshly grated nutmeg.

Traditionally, fresh beans are used for this recipe. However, the season for them is very short. If you can get them, you'll need to shell and peel them first. Frozen ones will work, but if they're large, they should be peeled before cooking. The easiest option is to use canned beans and that's what this *oma* does.

3 tbsp (45 g) butter

1 cup (150 g) diced onions

½ lb (227 g) lean slab bacon, cut into ½-inch (13-mm) cubes

3 tbsp (24 g) all-purpose flour

2 cups (500 ml) hot beef or vegetable broth

3 cups (500 g) canned broad beans, drained (see *Oma's Ecke*)

¼ tsp dried summer savory

Salt and freshly ground black pepper, as needed

Freshly grated nutmeg, as needed

2 tbsp (30 g) sour cream

2 tbsp (5 g) finely chopped fresh parsley, for garnish

Melt the butter in a large saucepan over medium heat. Add the onions and bacon and cook, stirring occasionally, until the bacon fat is rendered and the onions are translucent, 5 to 7 minutes. Dust the flour over the bacon and onions and stir until it has been absorbed. Slowly whisk in the broth, stirring until the sauce is creamy. If the sauce is too thick, add some water. Reduce the heat to low and simmer for 5 minutes, stirring occasionally.

Add the beans and summer savory to the sauce and simmer for 2 to 3 minutes to heat the beans thoroughly. Season with salt, pepper and nutmeg. Remove the saucepan from the heat and stir in the sour cream.

Serve the Dicke Bohnen und Speck garnished with the parsley.

Oma's Ecke

If you manage to find fresh broad beans, you'll first need to shell them by removing the beans from their pods. Cook the shelled beans in boiling water for 10 minutes, or until they're as tender as you like. Drain and shock them in ice water. Peel the outer membrane off each bean. You need about three times the quantity of fresh bean pods to get one quantity of final shelled beans.

If using frozen broad beans, cook them for about 5 minutes, or until tender. Do this by boiling them in salted water to which you've added the summer savory. To make the Dicke Bohnen und Speck, just follow the recipe above, but instead of the beef or vegetable broth, use the water that you boiled the beans in.

Kartoffelsalat ohne Mayo

(POTATO SALAD WITHOUT MAYO)

There's a culinary dividing line, which I call the "mayo line," between northern and southern Germany. Northerners mostly love using mayonnaise in their salads. Southerners usually do not. This Rhine region, being somewhat midway, enjoys both. Since the following salad has no mayo, it's the perfect one to take on a picnic or serve at a buffet. Even northern Germans, like me, love it.

Some people prefer to cook their potatoes the day before, peel them and refrigerate them. The following day, the hot dressing is added. This way, the potatoes hold their shape better. However, warm potatoes will absorb more of the dressing. It's a toss-up which way is best. Personally, I do mine all on the same day. That way, I don't need to plan ahead and can make the salad the day I'm craving it.

2 lbs (908 g) waxy potatoes or Yukon gold potatoes (see *Oma's Ecke*), unpeeled

1 tbsp (15 g) clarified butter or 1 tbsp (15 ml) neutral oil

5 oz (142 g) bacon, diced

¾ cup (115 g) finely diced onions

1 cup (250 ml) beef or vegetable broth

¼ cup (60 ml) white wine vinegar, plus more as needed

1 tsp mustard, plus more as needed

½ tsp salt, plus more as needed

¼ tsp freshly ground black pepper, plus more as needed

¼ tsp celery seeds

Sugar, as needed

2 tbsp (6 g) finely chopped fresh chives

To a large pot, add the potatoes, cover with water and cook over medium-high heat for 20 to 40 minutes, depending on their size. To check if they are tender, poke them with the point of a knife. It should slide in easily. Drain the potatoes, and rinse them under cold water to cool them slightly. Peel them while they are still warm. Cut them into ⅛- to ¼-inch (3- to 6-mm) slices and put them in a large serving bowl.

While the potatoes are cooking, melt the butter in a medium saucepan over medium heat. Add the bacon and onions and cook, stirring occasionally, until the bacon fat is rendered and the onions are translucent, 5 to 7 minutes. Stir in the broth and bring to a simmer. Remove the saucepan from the heat and stir in the vinegar, mustard, salt, pepper and celery seeds.

Pour the hot dressing over the sliced potatoes in the bowl and stir very gently. Let the salad rest for at least 20 to 30 minutes.

Gently mix the potatoes again and taste to check the seasonings. Add the sugar and additional salt, pepper, vinegar or mustard, if needed. Garnish with the chives just before serving.

Oma's Ecke

In Germany, one is blessed with many types of potatoes. Not so in other parts of the world. I was so thankful when Yukon golds became available at the markets. They work for almost every recipe.

Potatoes such as russets are high in starch and become fluffy when cooked, making them perfect for mashed potatoes. Waxy potatoes, such as red potatoes, with a low starch content and firm, creamy flesh, hold their shape well, making them perfect for potato salads. If you only have starchy potatoes available for salad, they'll still work. Just cut them into thicker slices so that they won't fall apart so easily.

Pfefferpotthast

(PEPPERED BEEF STEW)

The city of Dortmund, right in the middle of Nordrhein-Westfalen, has a yearly festival commemorating a 1378 victory that saved the city in which this stew played an important role. The *Pfefferpotthastfest* is celebrated every fall with the main food being, naturally, this stew.

"Peppered" here means "spiced," and that describes this Westphalian dish perfectly. Traditionally, the tender chunks of beef, braised in a rich, dark gravy, were served with boiled potatoes, gherkins and red beets. However, dumplings, Spätzle (Homemade Egg Noodles; page 60) or rice would be wonderful sides for this. Include a veggie, such as Blumenkohl mit Semmelbrösel (Cauliflower with Buttered Crumbs; page 110), and you have a feast!

3 tbsp (45 g) clarified butter or 3 tbsp (45 ml) neutral oil

1¾ lb (800 g) lean stewing beef, cut into ¾-inch (2-cm) cubes

1½ lbs (680 g) onions, cut into ¾-inch (2-cm) cubes

2 cups (500 ml) beef broth

¾ cup (108 g) diced dill pickles or gherkins

2 dried bay leaves

¼ tsp ground cloves

2 tbsp (19 g) cornstarch mixed with 2 tbsp (30 ml) cold water (see *Oma's Ecke*)

1 tbsp (15 ml) fresh lemon juice

½ tsp sugar

Salt and freshly ground black pepper, as needed

1 tbsp (9 g) capers

Melt the butter in a large saucepan over medium-high heat. Add one-third of the beef cubes and brown well on all sides, 5 to 8 minutes. Transfer the meat to a bowl. Continue browning the remaining beef cubes in batches, being careful not to crowd the meat.

Once all the beef has been browned, add the onions to the saucepan and sauté for 5 to 7 minutes, or until they are translucent. Add the broth, stirring to loosen any browned bits at the bottom of the saucepan. Transfer the meat and any accumulated juices from the bowl back to the saucepan. Add the pickles, bay leaves and cloves. Bring the mixture to a boil, reduce the heat to low, cover the saucepan and simmer for 1½ to 2 hours, or until the meat is very tender.

Stir in just enough of the cornstarch slurry to thicken the gravy during the last 5 minutes of simmering. Remove the bay leaves and season the stew with the lemon juice, sugar, salt, pepper and capers before serving.

Oma's Ecke

You'll notice that I frequently use cornstarch to thicken my sauces and gravies. I learned that from my *mutti*. Although it's more traditional to use flour, Mutti loved the cornstarch method. Why? Because as long as she dissolved the cornstarch in cold water, there were never, ever any lumps in her gravies.

Another great advantage is that the thickening happens immediately. You can slowly add the slurry, stirring and only adding as much as is needed. When using flour, lumps can occur and the thickening takes place over several minutes of cooking. It can be difficult to judge how much flour is needed.

The traditional way to thicken the *pfefferpotthast* was to add breadcrumbs. Sprinkle some dried breadcrumbs over the stew, stir and let it simmer for a minute before adding more. Giving the crumbs a bit of time to absorb the liquid will assure that you don't end up making it too thick.

Bayern

(Bavaria)

If you're adventuresome, then you must visit the largest state in Germany. You can climb the Berchtesgaden Alps, ski Zugspitze's glacier, trek through Franconia's vineyards, wander through Neuschwanstein Castle and shop Nuremberg's Christmas market. You can blend in with their beloved traditions: wear *lederhosen* or *dirndls*, participate in the breakneck sledge races during *Karneval*, climb the Maypole or join in the *schuhplattln*, a thigh-, sole- and hand-clapping rip-roaring folk dance.

Join the six million visitors who attend *Oktoberfest*, the largest beer festival in the world, in Munich for two weeks every year. Along with the ever-present beer, a banquet of ethnic foods is a scrumptious part of the celebration. These hearty foods, enjoyed by Bavarians throughout the whole year, are easy enough to make at home.

Schweinshaxn

(ROAST PORK HOCKS)

A trip to *Oktoberfest* in Munich undoubtedly means indulging in this showstopping, finger-licking, crispy-skinned, fall-off-the-bone meaty dish. A trip to *oma's* kitchen can be just as exciting since these can easily be made at home. These aren't at all like the pork hocks (also called knuckles) enjoyed by the Berliners (page 13). Those hocks are boiled and the fat layer removed to reveal ultra-juicy, tender chunks of meat. With these hocks' long roasting period, the crispy skin is the attraction. The challenge is to keep the meat juicy and tender as well. This recipe will do just that.

2 large onions, thickly sliced

3 large Cortland or Granny Smith apples, quartered

2 (1-lb [454-g]) fresh, meaty pork hocks (see *Oma's Ecke*)

1 tbsp (15 g) salt, plus more as needed

½ tsp freshly ground black pepper, plus more as needed

1 tsp caraway seeds

2 cups (500 ml) dark beer or water, plus more as needed

2 tbsp (19 g) cornstarch mixed with 2 tbsp (30 ml) cold water

Preheat the oven to 350°F (175°C).

Spread out the onions and apples in a large roasting pan.

With a sharp knife, score the skin and the fat layer of the pork, making the cuts about 1 inch (2.5 cm) apart, being careful not to cut into the meat. Massage the salt, pepper and caraway seeds over the skin and into the cuts. Stand the hocks in the roasting pan with the wide, fleshy part down and the narrow bone part up. Pour the beer around the hocks to a depth of about 1 inch (2.5 cm).

Roast the hocks in the oven for 3 to 4 hours, or until the skin is crispy and crackly, and the meat is fall-apart tender. In order to keep the meat moist and get the skin to crackling, keep the meaty ends submerged in the liquid yet the skin exposed to the dry oven heat. Add more beer, if needed, as the liquid evaporates. The internal temperature of the meat needs to be at least 165°F (74°C). Remove the roasting pan from the oven and place the hocks on a serving dish. Do not cover the hocks or the crispy skin will become soggy.

Strain the cooking liquid into a small saucepan over high heat. Bring the liquid to a simmer. Stir just enough of the cornstarch slurry into the simmering liquid to thicken the gravy. Season with additional salt and pepper. Serve this alongside the pork hocks. Serve with Semmelknödel (Bread Dumplings; page 59) and the sauerkraut from Sauerkraut und Bratwurst (Sauerkraut and Sausages; page 162) or simply rye bread, German *brötchen* (rolls) and Bavarian mustard.

Make sure you're using fresh pork hocks for this. Don't use the smoked ones. They'll not give you the crispy skin or the deliciously tender meat that the fresh ones do.

Brathendl

(ROAST CHICKEN)

If you've been to *Oktoberfest* in Munich, you'll probably have enjoyed feasting on their spit-grilled roasted chicken—crispy-skinned with moist, tender meat that's so finger-licking good. Grilling on a spit isn't something that's easily done at home, but using a butterflied (or a split and flattened) chicken makes the process of getting crispy skin and moist meat utterly easy.

Have the butcher prepare the bird for you or do it yourself. Either way, following this method, you'll also have some roasted potatoes ready to serve with your *brathendl*.

POTATOES

1 tbsp (15 ml) olive oil

1¾ lbs (800 g) peeled Yukon gold potatoes, cut into ½-inch (13-mm) thick slices

Salt, as needed

CHICKEN

2 tsp (10 g) salt

2 tsp (4 g) paprika

1 tsp freshly ground black pepper

3 tbsp (45 ml) melted butter

1 (3½-lb [1.6-kg]) whole chicken

Oma's Ecke

You can add thickly sliced onion rings, carrot slices and parsnips to the potatoes and have a roasted root vegetable medley to go along with the chicken. A nice variation—if not German, delicious!

Preheat the oven to 425°F (218°C).

To make the potatoes, brush a roasting pan with the oil. Put the potato slices in the pan in a single layer, turning them so that they are coated with the oil. Sprinkle the potatoes with salt. Place the pan's roasting rack over the potatoes.

To make the chicken, combine the salt, paprika and pepper in a small bowl. Pour in the melted butter and mix.

To butterfly the chicken, wash the bird inside and out under running water. Dry it thoroughly with paper towels. Lay the bird, breast-side down, with the legs facing you. Using poultry shears and starting at the cavity, cut along one side of the backbone. Turn the chicken around, and cut along the other side. Remove the backbone and set it aside to freeze it for making stock, if desired. Now, press down on each of the wings at the same time with the palms of your hands, until you hear the breastbone crack.

Brush the inside of the chicken with some of the butter mixture. Place the chicken, skin-side up, on the roasting rack and flatten it. Turn the legs outward to expose as much skin as possible. Tuck the wings underneath. Brush the remainder of the butter mixture over the chicken, making sure to get into the cracks between the legs and the breast.

Roast the chicken for 45 to 60 minutes, or until the internal temperature of the thighs is 170°F (77°C). Transfer the chicken to a serving plate and let it rest for 10 minutes before serving. Do not cover the bird or the crispy skin will soften. While the chicken is resting, flip the potatoes over and return them to the oven for 10 minutes to brown the other side.

Serve the chicken and potatoes with a green salad on the side.

Krautflecken mit Speck

(CABBAGE, NOODLES AND BACON)

My neighbor, Melania Orasch, introduced me to *krautflecken* many years ago. Since then, I've discovered that my friend's Austrian dish is also very popular in Germany, especially in the southern regions. For some people, including me, combining cabbage and noodles may seem strange. However, mix in some onion, butter, seasonings and perhaps some bacon, and that strange combination becomes a wonderful meal. Smoked sausage is a natural accompaniment for this.

2 tbsp (30 g) butter

2 cups (300 g) diced onions

3 oz (85 g) lean bacon, finely diced

2 cloves garlic, finely diced

2 lb (908 g) green cabbage, coarsely shredded

1 cup (250 ml) beef or vegetable broth, plus more as needed

1 (8-oz [225-g]) package wide egg noodles

1 tsp caraway seeds

Salt and freshly ground black pepper, as needed

1 to 2 tbsp (15 to 30 ml) pure white vinegar, optional

2 tbsp (5 g) finely chopped fresh parsley, for garnish

Melt the butter in a large saucepan over medium heat. Add the onions and bacon and cook, stirring occasionally, until the bacon fat is rendered and the onions are translucent, 5 to 7 minutes. Add the garlic and cabbage. Sauté for about 5 minutes, letting some of the cabbage brown. Stir in the broth. Bring the mixture to a boil, reduce the heat to medium-low, cover the saucepan and simmer for 25 minutes. Check occasionally to make sure that the liquid has not evaporated, adding extra broth or water if needed.

While the cabbage is cooking, prepare the egg noodles in a medium saucepan according to the package instructions, until just tender. Drain the noodles, cover the saucepan and set it aside.

When the cabbage is tender, add the caraway seeds and season the cabbage with salt and pepper. Stir in the vinegar (if using). Add the noodles and gently stir the mixture together.

Serve garnished with the parsley.

Oma's Ecke

Originally, this was considered *arme-leute-essen* (poor people's food) —a simple dish that was inexpensive and super simple to make. You can elevate this dish to an elegant status by mixing in 1 cup (230 g) of full-fat sour cream just before the noodles are stirred into the cabbage mixture.

The recipe as written is all that is needed for a nice light lunch. However, there are many variations you can make. Use savoy cabbage for a milder flavor. Add diced ham and grated cheese to make this a more substantial meal. Include marjoram as a seasoning. Garnish with caramelized onion rings. Add some diced tomatoes. Toss in some smoked sausage. So many variations are possible!

Schupfnudeln

(HOMEMADE POTATO NOODLES)

In Bavaria, there is a particularly delicious type of noodle that, when pan-fried, elevates the plain potato into a dish that's often served by itself. It's also the perfect accompaniment for pork, lamb, duck or sauerkraut, and when turned into dessert with cinnamon and applesauce, it's a fitting culmination of a traditional German meal.

Schupfen means "to push or throw." In this case, little bits of potato dough are rolled between the hands and thrown off into finger-shaped noodles, creating the classic shape of the ends narrower than the middle.

1½ lbs (680 g) peeled russet potatoes, quartered

2 tsp (10 g) salt, plus more as needed

4 tbsp (32 g) all-purpose flour, plus more for rolling (see *Oma's Ecke*)

2 large egg yolks

2 tbsp (19 g) potato starch or cornstarch

Freshly ground black pepper, as needed

Freshly ground nutmeg, as needed

2 tbsp (30 g) butter

Oma's Ecke

The exact amount of flour needed is impossible to predict. It depends wholly on the moisture content of the potatoes. Russets or other starchy potatoes, the best to use for this, will have differing amounts of moisture depending on the time of year. Add just enough flour to make a dough that doesn't stick to your hands.

Preheat the oven to 300°F (150°C) and set a 16 x 11–inch (40 x 28–cm) baking sheet near your workspace for easy access.

Put the potatoes in a large saucepan, cover them with water and bring them to a boil over high heat. Cover the saucepan, reduce the heat to medium-high and simmer until the potatoes are tender, about 20 minutes. Drain the potatoes and spread them onto the baking sheet. Place the baking sheet in the oven for 3 minutes to evaporate the moisture from the potatoes. Remove the baking sheet from the oven and let the potatoes cool slightly. Turn the oven off.

Fill a large pot with water, add the salt and bring the water to a boil over high heat. Cover the pot, reduce the heat to low and bring the water to a simmer. Dust a large plate with flour. Set the plate aside.

Mash the potatoes or press them through a potato ricer into a large bowl. Once they are cooled, add the egg yolks, flour and potato starch. Mix the ingredients together using your hands. Season the dough with additional salt, pepper and nutmeg. Transfer the dough to a floured work surface. Gently knead until the dough holds together and does not stick to your hands, adding extra flour as needed.

Divide the dough in half. Roll each half into a log about ½ inch (13 mm) thick. Cut each log into 1-inch (2.5-cm) pieces. Roll each piece between your hands into finger-size noodles with tapered ends and put them on the flour-dusted plate. Dust your hands with extra flour to keep the dough from sticking.

Fill a large bowl with cold water and set aside. Place a large empty bowl next to the bowl of water.

Drop half the noodles into the simmering salted water. When they rise to the surface, use a slotted spoon to place the noodles in the cold water to cool. Remove the noodles from the cold water and place them in the empty bowl.

Repeat this process with the remaining noodles. When all the noodles have been cooked, melt the butter in a large skillet over medium-high heat. Add the noodles and sauté for about 5 minutes, until they are golden brown, just before serving.

Bayrisch Weisskraut

(BAVARIAN CABBAGE)

Germans love their cabbage. Readily available, it's featured in many dishes, with the most popular being sauerkraut and red cabbage. In the Bavarian region, there's one variation that's even more desired, and this is it. Sweeter than a similar version made in northern Germany, this one is a good substitute for the sauerkraut in the Sauerkraut und Bratwurst (Sauerkraut and Sausages; page 162) and is a wonderful side dish for Schweinshaxn (Roast Pork Hocks; page 44).

3 tbsp (45 g) butter or bacon fat

1 large onion, thinly sliced

2 tbsp (24 g) sugar, plus more as needed

1 large Cortland or Granny Smith apple, peeled and thickly sliced

2 cups (500 ml) beef broth

1¾ to 2 lb (800 to 908 g) green cabbage, shredded

1 tsp caraway seeds (see *Oma's Ecke*)

1 tsp salt, plus more as needed

¼ tsp freshly ground black pepper, plus more as needed

Water, as needed

1 tbsp (15 ml) pure white vinegar, plus more as needed

2 tbsp (19 g) cornstarch mixed with 2 tbsp (30 ml) cold water, optional

Melt the butter in a large saucepan over medium heat. Add the onion and sugar. Sauté for about 5 minutes, stirring occasionally, until the onion is lightly caramelized, being careful that the onion does not burn. Add the apple and sauté for 1 minute.

Add the broth and stir up any browned bits from the bottom. Stir in the cabbage, caraway seeds, salt and pepper.

Reduce the heat to medium-low, bring the mixture to a simmer, cover the saucepan and cook for 45 to 60 minutes, or until the cabbage is tender, stirring occasionally and adding some water, if needed.

Stir in the vinegar and season with additional salt, pepper, sugar and vinegar.

If you wish to thicken the cooking liquid, stir just enough of the cornstarch slurry into the cabbage to get it as thick as you like and simmer for about 2 minutes before serving.

Oma's Ecke

Did you know that the caraway seeds are not just added for flavor? It seems that caraway seeds are a natural way to help reduce the gas problem that seems to follow some people when they eat cabbage.

Baden-Württemberg

Known as the Sunny Side of Germany and sharing borders with Switzerland and France, Baden-Württemberg's foods are influenced by its neighbors and totally beloved throughout the whole country. Baden-Württemberg is known for its gourmet restaurants using local ingredients, so a culinary tour to enjoy the cuisine may be just what you're yearning for.

After all that feasting, a trip to Europa-Park, Germany's biggest theme park; a walking tour of Mainau, the flower island in Lake Constance with one of the largest butterfly houses in Germany; a hike through the Black Forest; a shopping spree in the Outletcity Metzingen; and a race in a pumpkin regatta at Ludwigsburg Castle are perfect ways to get a bit of exercise. Then, when you're back in your own kitchen, you'll be ready to cook all the culinary treats that you enjoyed in Baden-Württemberg.

Krustenbraten

(ROAST PORK)

There are several ways to achieve crackling on a pork roast, but I find this one the easiest. It yields perfectly crisp crackling gracing the top of each slice of this wonderfully moist roast accompanied by a savory gravy. Best of all, this is actually quite a simple method for an extraordinary meal. Another name for this is *schweinsbraten*, simply meaning "pork roast," but the *krustenbraten* is more descriptive with the crispy *kruste*, or crust, that really is one of the reasons this dish is so loved.

Precooking the rind in the liquid for the first hour makes the rind soft and easy to cut through. When it's cut parallel to the grain and then in the opposite direction, it provides an easy guide for cutting the slices once it's roasted. Each piece ends up with a row of crispy crackling. Serve this with Semmelknödel (Bread Dumplings; page 59) and Bayrisch Weisskraut (Bavarian Cabbage; page 52). So, so good!

2 large carrots, thickly sliced

1 large leek, thickly sliced

2 large onions, thickly sliced

1 clove garlic, crushed

3 cups (750 ml) hot beef broth, plus more as needed

3 lb (1.4 kg) boneless pork shoulder with rind/fat cap (see *Oma's Ecke*)

1 tbsp (15 ml) oil

Salt and freshly ground black pepper, as needed

2 tbsp (19 g) cornstarch mixed with 2 tbsp (30 ml) cold water

2 tbsp (30 g) sour cream

Oma's Ecke

The roasting time at 325°F (163°C) is really dependent on the shape of the roast. A short and fat roast will take a bit longer than a long and skinny one. Also, every oven is different and may not be showing the proper temperature. That's why it's always important to check the internal temperature to make sure the roast is properly cooked.

Preheat the oven to 350°F (175°C).

Put the carrots, leek, onions and garlic in a 9 x 13–inch (23 x 33–cm) roasting pan. Pour the broth into the roasting pan and stir to mix in the garlic. Rub the pork shoulder with the oil and sprinkle it with salt and pepper. Place it in the roasting pan rind-side down so that the rind is submerged in the broth. Roast in the oven for 1 hour.

Remove the roast from the oven and reduce the heat to 325°F (163°C). Using a sharp knife, score through the rind (being careful not to cut into the meat) in 1-inch (2.5-cm) wide strips, in both directions. Place the meat, rind-side up, in the roasting pan so that the rind is not submerged in the liquid. Sprinkle the rind with additional salt and roast for 45 minutes, or until the internal temperature of the meat is at least 160°F (71°C), adding water as needed to keep the veggies from burning. If the rind is not crispy after this time, raise the temperature to 450°F (232°C) and roast for about 10 minutes. If needed, put it under the broiler to speed up the crisping, watching carefully that it does not burn.

Remove the pork shoulder from the roasting pan and set it aside to rest. Strain the cooking liquid into a small saucepan, pressing out as much liquid as possible from the veggies. Use a gravy separator if you wish to remove the fat. Add extra beef broth or water to make 2 cups (500 ml) of liquid. Bring to a simmer over medium-high heat and thicken with just enough cornstarch slurry to make a gravy. Cook for about 2 minutes. Remove the saucepan from the heat and stir in the sour cream. Season with salt and pepper. Serve the roast pork, sliced, with the gravy on the side.

Semmelknödel

(BREAD DUMPLINGS)

Centuries ago, in southern Germany and particularly in Baden-Württemberg, home cooks found a way to use stale *semmeln*, the Bavarian term for *brötchen* (rolls), to make a most delicious side dish: Semmelknödel. These were so good that today, they're even found in five-star restaurants.

Making these bread dumplings will take a good-quality bread (not a squishy sandwich loaf) and practice to get the feel for the right consistency. To check if the mixture is right, I always cook a test dumpling to make sure that it holds together. This gives me something yummy to nibble on as I wait for the rest to cook!

1 lb (454 g) stale bread or rolls

1½ cups (375 ml) hot milk

Hot water, as needed

1 tbsp (15 g) salt, plus more as needed

2 tbsp (30 g) butter

3 slices bacon, diced

½ cup (75 g) finely diced onions

½ tsp freshly grated nutmeg

2 tbsp (5 g) finely chopped fresh parsley, plus more for garnish

1 tsp dried marjoram, optional

Freshly ground black pepper, as needed

2 large eggs, lightly beaten

¼ cup (30 g) breadcrumbs or 2 tbsp (16 g) flour, if needed

Oma's Ecke

Eat these dumplings the way Germans do: tear them apart with your fork and never use your knife. The wonderfully rich gravy that accompanies most meat dishes is just waiting to be sopped up with these delicious morsels.

Thinly slice the bread or tear it into small pieces. Put the bread pieces in a large bowl. Pour the hot milk over the top. Stir gently and set aside to allow the bread to soak up the milk.

Fill a 5-quart (5-L) saucepan with hot water to within 2 inches (5 cm) of the top. Add the salt and bring to a boil over high heat. Reduce the heat to medium-low and bring the water to a slow simmer.

Meanwhile, melt the butter in a medium skillet over medium heat. Add the bacon and onions and cook for 8 to 10 minutes, stirring occasionally, until the bacon fat is rendered and the onions are golden. Add the skillet contents, including any fat, to the bread. Add the nutmeg, parsley and marjoram (if using) and mix gently.

Taste and adjust the salt and pepper, if needed. (This will depend on the saltiness of the bread and the bacon.) Add the eggs and, using your hands, gently mix until everything is evenly combined. If the mixture is too soft and sticky to form into balls, add the breadcrumbs, 1 tablespoon (8 g) at a time.

If this is your first time making these, make one dumpling and see how it turns out. Moisten your hands with cold water and make 1 (2-inch [5-cm]) dumpling.

Carefully drop the dumpling into the simmering water. If it falls apart as it is cooking, the dough is too dry. Adjust the remaining dough by adding a bit more milk. If it holds together, let it simmer for 15 to 20 minutes. Remove it with a slotted spoon and taste it. If it needs more salt or pepper, season the remaining dough.

Now form the rest of the dumplings and simmer them for 15 to 20 minutes, just like your test one. Remove the dumplings from the water and drain them briefly on paper towels. Put them on a serving platter and garnish them with additional parsley. Serve with gravy (see *Oma's Ecke*).

Spätzle

(HOMEMADE EGG NOODLES)

These little noodles, also called swabian noodles, are served with almost anything in Baden-Württemberg. Once commonly made at home, these are now available commercially, either dried or frozen. However, nothing beats homemade. The trickiest part is getting the dough the right consistency, since it is difficult to get *späzlemehl*, a finely ground, rough-textured flour, outside of Germany. Even with the right flour, its moisture content will be different according to the weather. Practice makes perfect. It sometimes takes several tries until you have perfected the consistency and the method. The result is totally worth the effort. After passing the learning curve, it really does become a quick and easy dish to make.

1 cup (125 g) all-purpose flour

1½ tsp (8 g) salt, divided

¼ tsp freshly grated nutmeg, optional

2 large eggs

¼ cup (60 ml) milk

2 tbsp (30 g) butter

In a large bowl, combine the flour, ½ teaspoon of the salt and nutmeg (if using). In a small bowl, whisk the eggs and milk. Pour this mixture over the flour. Mix and then beat with a wooden spoon until the dough is smooth. It should be the consistency of a very thick pancake batter. If it is too thick, add more milk. Let the dough rest for 15 minutes.

Fill a 5-quart (5-L) saucepan with hot water to within 2 inches (5 cm) of the top. Add 1 teaspoon of the salt and bring the water to a boil over high heat. Reduce the heat to medium-low and bring the water to a gentle simmer. Melt the butter in a medium skillet over medium-high heat and set it aside. Have a colander ready to drain the cooked *spätzle*.

Using a *spätzle* press, potato ricer or another metal colander, press the dough through the holes into the simmering water. Do this in several batches. Cook the noodles for 1 to 2 minutes, or until they float to the top, stirring once or twice to prevent them from sticking to each other.

Remove the noodles with a slotted spoon and put them in the colander to drain. When they are all cooked, put the skillet over medium heat and toss the noodles in the butter. Sauté for 2 to 5 minutes, either just to coat the noodles or to brown them slightly. Serve immediately.

Want to make these *spätzle* entirely traditionally? Instead of using a kitchen gadget, use a wooden cutting board and a long-bladed knife. Here's how: Wet the board, put a spoonful of dough on it, spread it into a thin layer with the knife blade, hold the board over the pot with the simmering water and, first dipping the knife into the boiling water, scrape small pieces of dough into the water. Keep wetting the knife and the edge of the board with water right out of the pot as you scrape off the noodles. You will soon develop a rhythm as you scrape and dip. Your pot of noodles will fill up quickly.

Käsespätzle

(CHEESE NOODLE CASSEROLE)

Spätzle (Homemade Egg Noodles; page 60), those wonderful little noodles that the Baden-Württemberg area is so famous for, find their way here into a German version of mac and cheese. Although *spätzle* are considered noodles, they really are more like pasta, so they work very well for this. Whether your *spätzle* are long, skinny ones, or more like the Swiss *knöpfle* (which are rounded little bits of pasta), they can easily be turned into this creamy dish.

It's not known when or who the first person was to think that layering *spätzle* with cheese and adding caramelized onions would be so delicious, but this dish is among the most popular in the region. It's often served with just a green salad or bowl of applesauce. If, and that is a big if, you happen to have leftovers, fry them in butter the next day for another treat.

CASSEROLE

4 tbsp (60 g) butter, divided

2 large onions, thinly sliced

4 cups (360 g) cooked Spätzle (Homemade Egg Noodles; page 60), warm (see *Oma's Ecke*)

2 to 3 cups (240 to 360 g) shredded Emmental cheese

CARAMELIZED ONION GARNISH

1 tbsp (15 g) clarified butter or 1 tbsp (15 ml) neutral oil

1 large onion, sliced into thick rings

Preheat the oven to 400°F (200°C). Use 1 tablespoon (15 g) of the butter to grease a 9 x 13-inch (23 x 33-cm) casserole dish.

To make the casserole, melt the remaining 3 tablespoons (45 g) of the butter in a large skillet over medium heat. Add the onions and sauté until they are lightly caramelized, about 10 minutes. Reduce the heat if they brown too quickly.

Spread half of the *spätzle* in the casserole dish. Layer half the cheese and half the onions over the noodles. Cover this layer with the remaining *spätzle* and finish layering with the remaining onions and cheese.

Bake the casserole, uncovered, for 15 to 20 minutes, or until the top is bubbly and lightly browned.

Meanwhile, prepare the caramelized onion garnish by melting the butter in a large skillet over medium-low heat. Sauté the onion slowly until it is caramelized, about 10 to 15 minutes. Stir occasionally to keep it from sticking.

Serve the Käsespätzle right from the casserole dish, garnished with the caramelized onion rings.

Oma's Ecke

If you're using leftover *spätzle* that are cold from the fridge, let them warm up to room temperature or spread them out in the greased casserole dish and cover it with foil. Put the casserole in the oven as it's preheating. The *spätzle* should be warm enough once the oven is at the right temperature. Take the casserole dish out of the oven and transfer half the *spätzle* to a bowl. Layer the cheese and onions, cover that layer with the remaining *spätzle* and finish as directed in the recipe.

Gaisburger Marsch

(BEEF AND VEGGIE STEW)

There are interesting stories that discuss the origin of this nineteenth-century dish from Gaisburg, a district of Stuttgart in Baden-Württemberg. There's talk of soldiers, prisoners and wives marching in order to enjoy this hearty stew. Since that time, many variations for this recipe have arisen, including mine. What they all have in common is a very flavorful beef broth.

This is a wonderful soup to make when you have leftover roast beef. To make it from scratch, use the recipe for Tafelspitz mit Meerrettich-Sosse (Boiled Beef with Horseradish Sauce; page 148) for the meat and the broth, perhaps adding extra soup bones to increase the flavor. Either way, you'll be having a meal fit for everyone, including those soldiers.

6 cups (1.5 L) beef broth (see *Oma's Ecke*)

1 lb (454 g) peeled Yukon gold potatoes, cut into ½-inch (13-mm) cubes

½ lb (227 g) carrots, cut into ½-inch (13-mm) cubes

1 large rib celery, cut into ½-inch (13-mm) cubes

6 oz (170 g) uncooked egg noodles or dried packaged *spätzle* (see *Oma's Ecke*)

2 tbsp (30 g) butter

1 medium onion, thinly sliced

1 lb (454 g) cooked roast beef, cut into ½-inch (13-mm) cubes

Salt and freshly ground black pepper, as needed

MAGGI® Liquid Seasoning, optional (see *Oma's Ecke*)

2 tbsp (5 g) finely chopped fresh parsley, for garnish

Pour the broth into a large saucepan over high heat. Add the potatoes, carrots and celery and bring the vegetables to a boil. Reduce the heat to medium-low, cover the saucepan and simmer for 5 minutes. Add the noodles and simmer for 10 minutes, or until the vegetables and noodles are tender.

Meanwhile, melt the butter in a medium skillet over medium heat. Add the onion and sauté until it is caramelized, about 10 minutes.

When the vegetables are tender, add the roast beef to the soup and season with salt, pepper and MAGGI (if using). Simmer for 2 to 3 minutes to heat the meat.

To serve, ladle the stew into soup bowls and garnish each serving with the caramelized onions and parsley.

Oma's Ecke

The traditional recipe for this stew is done totally from scratch. That means the first step is to make that delicious broth and tender beef. However, to speed things up, using a purchased broth is fine. Just make sure you get the best you can and increase the flavor by seasoning carefully. Alternatively, you could make a homemade broth ahead of time and freeze to use for soups.

If the noodles you are using require a shorter cooking time, adjust when you add them to the soup so that they'll be cooked when the veggies are done. Alternatively, you can cook the noodles separately and add them to the finished soup. That way, there is no chance of overcooking them.

MAGGI Liquid Seasoning is a traditional seasoning used throughout Germany. It is similar to soy sauce, perhaps with a touch of Worcestershire sauce, but it has a deeper, richer and saltier taste. Alternatively, if you have access to lovage, also called the MAGGI plant, you can add a few leaves. No MAGGI or lovage? Season the stew with salt and pepper, perhaps adding a few drops of soy sauce.

Niedersachs
(lower saxony)

If you're wanting an out-of-the-ordinary holiday, you've chosen the right state. Race across the Wadden Sea's tidal flats in special *schlickschlitten* (mud sleds) during the annual *Ostfriesischen Wattspiele* (East Frisian mudflat games). Navigate over twenty rivers by kayak or immerse yourself in the saltwater thermal baths in Lüneburg. Visit the world's largest bird park, Weltvogelpark Walsrode, right in the middle of the Lüneburg Heath. Participate in Hannover's *Schützenfest* (marksmen festival), even if just by indulging at the dozens of snack bars. Join the two million visitors at the Maschsee Lake Festival, Germany's biggest open-air arena with music, entertainment and culinary specialties.

Then, of course, there's the Pied Piper and his rats . . . that's what I think of as well when Lower Saxony comes to mind. This region is known for its gourmet food: duck, lamb and, yes, rat tails! Delicious food awaits you here.

Gebratene Ente

(ROAST DUCK)

Christmas often means that a special roast is on the menu. For many, it's a roast goose, but duck is often a delicious substitute. Usually easier to find and less expensive, duck—with its heartier and richer flavor—makes its appearance on many tables at this time of year. There are so many ways to prepare it, but sometimes the simplest is the best. Having an elegant, festive dish that's easy to make and delicious makes this *oma* happy.

Make sure you keep the "liquid gold" that's left in the roasting pan. Duck fat is considered among the healthiest of all animal fats (including butter). It's perfect for frying potatoes, adding to veggies and searing meats.

1 (5-lb [2.3-kg]) duck (see *Oma's Ecke*)

1 tsp salt

½ tsp freshly ground black pepper

½ tsp paprika

1 small Cortland or Granny Smith apple, unpeeled and quartered (see *Oma's Ecke*)

1 medium rib celery, coarsely chopped

1 small onion, unpeeled and quartered (see *Oma's Ecke*)

Preheat the oven to 400°F (200°C). Set a metal skewer, some kitchen twine and a medium roasting pan with a rack near your workspace for easy access.

Prepare the duck by making sure the cavity is empty of giblets, removing any fat from inside and trimming the skin at the neck, leaving just enough to be able to close the neck cavity. Check that there are no feather quills sticking out of the skin. If there are, pull them out with tweezers. You can also cut off the wing tips, if you wish. Rinse the duck inside and out under cold running water. Pat the bird dry with paper towels.

In a small bowl, combine the salt, pepper and paprika. Sprinkle the inside and outside of the duck with this seasoning mix. Stuff the duck's cavity with the apple, celery and onion. Fold the flap of neck skin to cover the cavity and secure with the skewer. Using kitchen twine, tie the legs together. Place the duck on the rack of a roasting pan breast-side up.

Roast the duck in the oven for 1 hour. Lower the temperature to 325°F (163°C). Baste the duck with the pan juices and roast until the duck's internal thigh temperature reaches 165°F (74°C) and the leg joints move freely, about 1 hour. Remove the roasting pan from the oven and place the duck on a serving dish. Loosely tent it with foil and let it sit for 10 minutes before serving. Remember to remove the skewer and the twine. Carve and serve.

Oma's Ecke

There are two schools of thought in roasting a duck: one is that the skin needs to be pricked before roasting and the other thinks it does not. You may want to try both ways to see which you prefer. If you do decide to prick the skin, make sure you don't pierce the meat. To avoid piercing the meat, poke a skewer into the skin at an angle, rather than straight down.

Leaving the skins on the apples and onions increases the flavors that they release. Just make sure they're washed clean before using them.

Gulaschsuppe

(GOULASH SOUP)

The first place I had goulash soup was at a rest stop along the *autobahn* (highway) in Lower Saxony. The buffet in the restaurant was extensive, but that goulash soup spoke to me. It was so delicious that I had to find a recipe to match it once I got home. I had made my own version previously by just adding potatoes and green beans to my goulash recipe. This *gulaschsuppe*, however, was different. With the peppers and seasonings, it's become a dish I now often serve to guests.

Goulash originated in Hungary but has been adopted as traditional German fare. Once you taste this soup, you'll understand why. Serve this with some freshly baked German bread. Nothing else is needed.

2 tbsp (30 g) clarified butter or 2 tbsp (30 ml) neutral oil

1 lb (454 g) stewing beef, cut into ¾-inch (2-cm) cubes

2 cups (300 g) diced onions

1 clove garlic, crushed

1 large rib celery, diced

1 large carrot, cut into ½-inch (13-mm) slices

1 tbsp (16 g) tomato paste

1½ cups (375 ml) tomato juice

1 cup (250 ml) beef broth

1 tsp salt, plus more as needed

1 tbsp (6 g) sweet Hungarian paprika

1 dried bay leaf

1 lb (454 g) Yukon gold potatoes, cut into ¾-inch (2-cm) cubes

3 medium bell peppers (preferably different colors), cut into ¾-inch (2-cm) pieces

Freshly ground black pepper, as needed

Hot Hungarian paprika, as needed

2 tbsp (5 g) finely chopped fresh parsley, for garnish

Melt the butter in a large saucepan over medium-high heat. Add about one-third of the beef, being careful not to crowd the saucepan, and brown it well on all sides, 5 to 8 minutes. Transfer the beef to a medium bowl. Brown the rest of the beef in batches.

Reduce the heat to medium and add the onions. Sauté for 5 to 7 minutes, stirring often. Stir in the garlic, celery, carrot and tomato paste and sauté for 2 minutes. Return all the meat to the saucepan along with any accumulated juices. Stir in the tomato juice, beef broth, salt, sweet Hungarian paprika and bay leaf. Reduce the heat to medium-low, cover the saucepan and simmer for 45 minutes.

Add the potatoes and bell peppers. Simmer for 15 minutes, or until the potatoes are tender. Remove the bay leaf. Season with additional salt, pepper and the hot Hungarian paprika.

Serve garnished with the parsley.

Oma's Ecke

Whenever you're browning vegetables, such as onions, celery and carrots, you may find the bottom of the pot is starting to get too dark with the browned bits sticking to it. Add a little bit of liquid, stir to scrape the browned bits into the liquid, lower the heat if needed and let the liquid evaporate. The veggies will return to sautéing and a deeper flavor will develop. You may need to add a bit more butter or oil. This browning, adding liquid, evaporating and continuing to brown is a technique to get a really dark and flavorful stock for gravies or soups.

Hamelner Rattenschwänze

(HAMELIN "RAT TAILS")

When you visit Hamelin in Lower Saxony, you'll know right away that you've arrived in the Pied Piper's town. The *glockenspiel* (carillon) at the Hochzeitshaus (Wedding House) recounts the sinister tale. Restaurants join in by offering their famous *rattenschwänze* for dinner. Using pork strips flambéed at your table, nestled among veggies in a rich wine gravy and served over a bed of rice, these "tails" are a yummy end to a day of touristy travels.

The actual recipe is a secret, so I'm using culinary license and giving a child-friendly version with chicken and omitting the apple brandy and wine, just like an *oma* would do.

1½ lbs (680 g) boneless chicken breasts

4 tbsp (60 g) clarified butter or 4 tbsp (60 ml) neutral oil, divided

Salt and freshly ground black pepper, as needed

1 cup (150 g) diced onions

20 small button mushrooms

1 medium red bell pepper, cut into thin strips

1 medium green bell pepper, cut into thin strips

¼ cup (60 ml) apple juice (see *Oma's Ecke*)

2 medium tomatoes, peeled and cut into ½-inch (13-mm) pieces

1 (10-oz [280-g]) can baby corn, drained

1½ cups (375 ml) beef broth

1 tbsp (15 g) German whole-grain mustard

3 tbsp (28 g) cornstarch mixed with 3 tbsp (45 ml) cold water

¼ cup (60 ml) heavy cream

Cut the chicken breasts into long, thin strips. Melt 2 tablespoons (30 g) of the butter in a large skillet over medium-high heat. Add the chicken strips and sauté for about 5 minutes, or until the chicken is cooked through and lightly browned. Transfer the chicken to a plate and season it with salt and pepper. Cover the chicken to keep it warm.

Melt the remaining 2 tablespoons (30 g) of the butter in the skillet over medium heat. Add the onions and cook for 5 to 7 minutes, or until they are tender but not browned. Add the mushrooms, red bell pepper and green bell pepper. Fry for 5 minutes. Add the apple juice and stir to loosen any brown bits on the bottom of the skillet.

Add the tomatoes and baby corn. Stir and simmer for 5 minutes, letting the liquid evaporate. Add the broth and stir in the mustard. Return to a simmer. Stir in just enough of the cornstarch slurry to thicken the gravy. Season with salt and pepper. Remove the skillet from the heat and stir in the cream.

Return the chicken to the sauce and let it sit for several minutes to heat through before serving.

Oma's Ecke

The original recipe uses pork loin that's flambéed at the table with Calvados (an apple brandy), hence the use of apple juice in mine. The sauce also has olives, Worcestershire sauce and Tabasco, as well as ¼ cup (60 ml) each of white wine, red wine and port (which I've replaced with beef broth). These aren't really child-friendly ingredients, so I've omitted them from my version, but if you want to include them, by all means do.

Hammelfleisch Eintopf

(LAMB STEW)

Eintopf means "one pot," which totally describes what this stew is. Made in one pot and simmered to perfection, it's an easy way to bring a warming dish to your family. In Lower Saxony, this dish usually includes lamb, since the *heidschnucke* (a type of sheep) are pastured on the Lüneburg Heath, a popular tourist destination in this region.

Although lamb isn't as commonly eaten in Germany as pork and beef, it's often enjoyed with green beans, a perfect complement, as in this traditional *eintopf*.

2 tbsp (30 g) clarified butter or
2 tbsp (30 ml) neutral oil

1½ lbs (680 g) boneless lamb, cut into
¾-inch (2-cm) cubes (see *Oma's Ecke*)

1 large onion, thinly sliced

3 cups (750 ml) beef broth

1½ lbs (680 g) fresh green beans,
ends trimmed and cut in half (see
Oma's Ecke)

1½ lbs (680 g) peeled Yukon gold
potatoes, cut into 1-inch (2.5-cm)
cubes

1 tbsp (3 g) finely chopped fresh
summer savory (see *Oma's Ecke*)

Salt and freshly ground black pepper,
as needed

4 tbsp (60 g) sour cream, for garnish

1 tbsp (3 g) finely chopped fresh
parsley, for garnish

Melt the butter in a large saucepan over medium-high heat. Add one-third of the lamb, being careful not to crowd the saucepan, and brown well on all sides, 5 to 8 minutes. Transfer the meat to a medium bowl. Continue browning the rest of the lamb in batches.

Add the onion to the saucepan and sauté for 5 to 7 minutes, or until it is tender. Add the broth, stirring to loosen any browned bits at the bottom of the saucepan. Return the lamb to the saucepan along with any accumulated juices. Bring the mixture to a boil, reduce the heat to medium-low, cover the saucepan and simmer for 30 minutes.

Add the green beans and potatoes, increase the heat to high and bring the mixture back to a boil. Reduce the heat to medium-low, cover the saucepan and simmer for 30 minutes, or until the vegetables and meat are tender.

Add the summer savory and season with salt and pepper. Serve the stew in soup bowls with a dollop of sour cream and garnished with the parsley.

Oma's Ecke

If you don't like lamb or can't find it at the butcher, you can substitute beef, pork or sausage in this recipe. If you want an easier and quicker option, use frozen green beans, which you would add for the last 20 minutes of cooking time.

Summer savory is called *bohnenkraut* in Germany. The literal translation for this is "bean herb," since it amplifies the green beans' flavor. If you don't have fresh available, you can use dried. For most herbs, 1 tablespoon (15 g) of fresh equals 1 teaspoon (5 g) of dried.

Himmel und Erde

("HEAVEN AND EARTH"—APPLES AND POTATOES)

Fruit from the heavens (apples) and fruit from the earth (potatoes) describe what *Himmel und Erde* (Heaven and Earth) are. When these two are mixed together, they create a rather unusual dish that is a wonderful side to many meats. This comfort food can be served chunky or mashed. If you want it chunky, you'll need to cook each separately and then mix them together. Mashed is easier. Cooking the apples and potatoes together in one pot and mashing makes this super quick. Traditionally, *Himmel und Erde* is served with fried blood sausage; however, it is really good alongside any grilled sausage or pork dishes.

4 tbsp (60 g) butter, divided

4 oz (112 g) bacon, diced (see *Oma's Ecke*)

2 large onions, thickly sliced

1½ lbs (680 g) peeled russet potatoes, cubed

1 lb (454 g) Cortland or Granny Smith apples, peeled and thickly sliced (see *Oma's Ecke*)

1 tsp salt

¾ cup (175 ml) hot milk, or as needed

Salt and freshly ground black pepper, as needed

Freshly grated nutmeg, as needed

Melt 1 tablespoon (15 g) of the butter in a large skillet over medium heat. Add the bacon and fry for about 8 minutes, until the fat is rendered and the bacon is crispy. Transfer the bacon to paper towels to absorb the grease. Add the onions to the bacon fat in the skillet with 1 tablespoon (15 g) of the butter. Sauté until the onions are caramelized, about 10 minutes, reducing the heat if they brown too quickly.

Meanwhile, put the potatoes and apples in a large saucepan, cover them with water, add the salt and bring them to a boil over high heat. Reduce the heat to medium-low, cover the saucepan and simmer for 10 to 15 minutes, or until the potatoes and apples are tender. Drain and add the remaining 2 tablespoons (30 g) of the butter. Using a potato masher and adding as much milk as necessary, mash the potatoes and apples until they are smooth and creamy. Season with salt, pepper and nutmeg.

Serve the *Himmel und Erde* topped with the crispy bacon and caramelized onions.

Oma's Ecke

If you prefer, stir the bacon into the potato mixture. Don't want the bacon? Leave it out completely. For an interesting variation, use a mixture of apples and pears cooked together with the potatoes.

This method of mixing fruit with the potatoes can be changed to include vegetables instead. Cooked kale is a common addition. It's a great way to get kids to eat their greens. Cooked carrots are another favorite veggie that's frequently mashed in with the potatoes, resulting in a pretty orange color. These could all be classified as "baby food" but are really just delicious renditions of plain mashed potatoes.

Rheinland Pfalz

(Rhineland-Palatinate)

If you're wanting the unusual, then forge your own path and visit the oldest city in Germany, Trier, founded by the Celts before the first century BC. Roam through its nine UNESCO World Heritage sites before heading to Deidesheim to participate in the shenanigans at the historical *geissbock* (billy goat) auction that goes all the way back to 1404.

Then do the usual thing. Take at least one cruise down the picturesque Rhine or Moselle. There are castles at almost every bend, terraced vineyards reaching high up the slopes and fairy-tale villages along the banks. Stop off in Bad Dürkheim for one of the world's largest wine festivals, dating back to 1417, and see if you can figure out why it's called the *wurstmarkt* (sausage market).

Another must is stopping at a local *gaststätte* (restaurant). You'll find so many enticing and mouthwatering items on the menu, you'll be eager to cook them all once you are back home.

Sauerbraten mit Rosinen

(MARINATED BEEF WITH RAISINS)

Sauerbraten is enjoyed throughout Germany. In this region, there's an interesting twist: raisins. Providing a touch of sweetness, they're added to the sauce right at the end. Of course, Schneebällchen (Potato Dumplings from Cooked Potatoes; page 84) and Apfel-Rotkohl (Red Cabbage with Apples; page 184) are the perfect sides, as is the traditional applesauce. The wonderful flavor and tenderness of this meat is dependent on the long marinating process. For the best results, start this about three to five days before you want to cook the meat.

MARINADE

1 cup (250 ml) dry red wine

¼ cup (60 ml) red wine vinegar

½ cup (125 ml) water

1 medium onion, quartered

1 large carrot, cut into 1-inch (2.5-cm) pieces

1 dried bay leaf

1 allspice berry, crushed

½ tsp mustard seeds

½ tsp crushed black peppercorns

½ tsp crushed juniper berries

ROAST

2 lb (908 g) beef rump, chuck or bottom round roast

Salt and freshly ground black pepper, as needed

3 tbsp (45 g) clarified butter or 3 tbsp (45 ml) neutral oil, divided

1 large carrot, diced

1 cup (150 g) diced onions

½ cup (125 ml) beef broth

1½ cups (375 ml) reserved marinade

⅓ cup (50 g) raisins

2 tbsp (19 g) cornstarch mixed with 2 tbsp (30 ml) cold water (see *Oma's Ecke*)

Pinch of sugar

To make the marinade, combine the wine, vinegar, water, onion, carrot, bay leaf, allspice berry, mustard seeds, peppercorns and juniper berries in a large saucepan. Bring to a boil over high heat. Remove the saucepan from the heat and let the marinade cool.

To make the roast, put the beef in a resealable freezer bag. You can also use a glass or ceramic bowl that is just big enough for the meat and marinade. Pour the cooled marinade over the meat. Seal the bag. If you are using a bowl and there is not enough liquid to cover the meat, add some water. Cover the bowl tightly with plastic wrap. Refrigerate the beef for 3 to 5 days, turning it over twice a day. Remove the beef and strain the marinade into a large bowl, reserving it. Dry the meat completely with paper towels and sprinkle it with salt and pepper.

Melt 2 tablespoons (30 g) of the butter in a large saucepan over medium-high heat. Brown the meat for about 2 minutes on each side. Transfer the meat to a plate. Add the remaining 1 tablespoon (15 g) of the butter, lower the heat to medium and add the carrot and onions to the saucepan. Sauté for 5 minutes, or until the vegetables are slightly softened. Add the broth and the reserved marinade, stirring up the browned bits on the bottom of the saucepan. Return the meat to the saucepan, lower the heat to low, cover the saucepan and simmer for 2 to 3 hours, or until the meat is tender.

Transfer the beef to a platter and tent it with foil to keep it warm. Strain the cooking liquid through a sieve and return it to the saucepan. Add the raisins and bring the mixture to a simmer. Stir just enough of the cornstarch slurry into the simmering liquid to thicken the gravy. Season with the sugar and additional salt and pepper. Serve the meat, sliced, with the gravy on the side.

Oma's Ecke

In Germany, you can buy *lebkuchen* cookies that are sold specifically to add spiciness and thickening to this sauce. If you'd like to try that, add ½ cup (45 g) of crushed gingersnap cookies instead of the cornstarch slurry to this recipe.

Döppekooche

(POTATO CASSEROLE WITH BACON)

Going by several names, such as *kesselsknall*, *uhles* and *topfkuchen*, this potato dish is similar to scalloped potatoes but made more flavorful with the addition of bacon. To add even more flavor, sliced *mettwurst* (raw smoked pork sausage) is added. Since this isn't readily available outside of Germany, it can be replaced with your favorite smoked sausage. *Döppekooche* is a meal in itself. All that's needed is a green salad and a traditional side of homemade applesauce.

3 lbs (1.4 kg) peeled Yukon gold potatoes

2 tbsp (30 g) clarified butter or 2 tbsp (30 ml) neutral oil

4 oz (112 g) bacon, diced

2 cups (300 g) diced onions

2 large eggs

1 tsp salt

1 lb (454 g) smoked sausage, cut into ¼-inch (6-mm) slices

Preheat the oven to 375°F (190°C). Grease a 9 x 13-inch (23 x 33-cm) casserole dish.

Grate the potatoes and put them into a sieve over a bowl. Press down on the potatoes to remove as much water as possible. Let them drain for 10 to 15 minutes, pressing down occasionally.

Meanwhile, melt the butter in a medium skillet over medium heat. Add the bacon and onions and sauté, stirring occasionally, for about 5 minutes, until the bacon fat has rendered and the onions are lightly caramelized. Set aside to cool.

Carefully pour the liquid out of the bowl that is under the potatoes, keeping the starch that has settled on the bottom of the bowl. Scrape up that starch to loosen it, add the grated potatoes, eggs, salt and the bacon-onion mixture. Mix everything together using your hands. When the ingredients are thoroughly mixed, add the sausage slices. Put the mixture in the casserole dish, pressing down to level the top.

Bake the casserole for about 1½ hours. If the top is getting too dark, cover it with foil. Test for doneness by inserting a wooden toothpick into the center. Nothing should stick to the toothpick when you remove it. The top of the Döppekooche should be nicely browned and crisp. Serve hot.

Oma's Ecke

There are many regional dishes that are now enjoyed throughout all of Germany, perhaps with slight changes that reflect the region one is in. Examples of this would be rouladen or sauerkraut. This dish from the Rhineland-Palatinate isn't one of these. *Döppekooche* has remained a truly local dish that many Germans in other parts of the country have never even heard of.

Schneebällchen

(POTATO DUMPLINGS FROM COOKED POTATOES)

Snowballs, as they are known in the Palatinate region, or *kartoffelknödel* or *kartoffelklösse* in most other regions, are dumplings made from cooked potatoes. Ideally, the potatoes should be cooked and riced the day before you make this dish in order to get a fluffier dumpling. If you really want them today, just cool the riced potatoes in the fridge as long as you can before you start making the dumplings.

These dumplings are wonderful served with beef, pork or turkey, especially when there's a lot of gravy. Leftovers can be sliced and fried in butter for a delicious and easy lunch the next day.

2¼ lbs (1 kg) russet potatoes, washed and unpeeled

1½ tsp (8 g) salt, divided

1⅓ cups (213 g) potato flour or cornstarch, divided

2 large eggs

Pinch of freshly grated nutmeg

Oma's Ecke

Ideally, a potato ricer is the best tool to use here. It makes a fluffier "mashed" potato and is actually the preferred way to make mashed potatoes. If you don't have a ricer, you can use a potato masher, but try to be gentle and create a fluffy mash. Don't use a mixer. It'll create a gummy mash that will produce gummy dumplings.

If you have croutons, tuck one or two into the middle of each dumpling as you're forming them. They add a lovely flavor and texture and assure that there's no uncooked center in the dumpling. Use store-bought salad croutons or fry cubes of bread in butter until they are toasty brown.

Prepare the potatoes by putting them in a large pot, covering them with cold water and bringing them to a boil over high heat. Reduce the heat to medium-low to bring the water to a gentle boil, cover the pot and cook until the potatoes are tender, 20 to 40 minutes, depending on their size. Check that the potatoes can be easily pierced with a knife. Drain the potatoes, rinse them briefly under cold water and let them cool slightly. Peel them and press the warm potatoes through a potato ricer into a large bowl. Let the riced potatoes cool completely, cover the bowl and refrigerate the potatoes overnight.

When you are ready to make the dumplings, fill a large pot with water and add 1 teaspoon of the salt. Bring the water to a boil over high heat. Cover the pot, reduce the heat to medium-low and bring the water to a simmer.

Add 1 cup (160 g) of the flour, the eggs, the remaining ½ teaspoon of salt and the nutmeg to the riced potatoes. Mix well using your hands. Add the remaining ⅓ cup (53 g) of flour, as needed, in order to get a smooth dough. Lightly flour a work surface and transfer the dough to the work surface. Dip your hands into a bit of flour and then knead the dough very gently until it holds together.

It is a good practice to always make a test dumpling. Take ¼ cup (60 g) of the dough and form it into a ball with your floured hands. Drop it gently into the simmering water. Cook 10 to 15 minutes, uncovered, until the test dumpling floats to the surface. If it falls apart as it is cooking, add a bit more flour to the dough. Remove the test dumpling with a slotted spoon and see if it is cooked through.

Form the rest of the dough into a thick log. Cut it into 12 to 14 equal pieces. Form each piece into a ball and cook, uncovered, for 10 to 15 minutes in the simmering water. Remove the dumplings with a slotted spoon and place them on a serving plate. Serve immediately.

Kartoffelpuffer

(POTATO PANCAKES)

Called *grumbeerpannekuche* in Rhineland-Palatinate and *reibekuchen* or *kartoffelpfannkuchen* in other regions, potato pancakes are frequently enjoyed at street stalls, Christmas markets and especially during *karneval*. One reason for this is that many Germans don't like to make these delicious treats themselves at home—the frying smell seems to linger in the house. However, I find that when using clarified butter, it smells delicious. There is nothing quite like enjoying these potato pancakes right out of the pan and making them just like Oma.

2½ lbs (1.1 kg) peeled starchy potatoes (such as russets), finely grated

1 medium onion, finely grated

3 large eggs

1 tsp salt

⅓ cup (50 g) all-purpose flour

½ cup (120 g) clarified butter or ½ cup (125 ml) neutral oil, divided

Ensure that the grated potatoes are quite dry. You can put them in a sieve over a bowl to drain for at least 1 hour, pressing on them with a wooden spoon from time to time; or you can put them in a clean dish towel, bring the corners together and twist to squeeze as much liquid out of the potatoes as possible.

Preheat the oven to 250°F (121°C). Put a large baking sheet in the oven. Put a paper towel on a plate near the stove.

In a large bowl, mix together the potatoes, onion, eggs, salt and flour.

Melt ¼ cup (60 g) of the butter in a large skillet over medium-high heat. Using a large spoon or ladle (depending on the size of the pancakes you want), scoop the potato mixture into the skillet, pressing down to flatten the pancakes. Make sure that the pancakes do not touch one another. Cook for 2 to 5 minutes, then carefully flip the pancakes over when the edges have become browned. Cook for 2 to 5 minutes, and once the other side has browned, transfer the pancakes to the paper towel to drain. After they have drained, put them on the baking sheet in the oven to keep them warm.

Repeat this process until all the potato mixture is used, adding the remaining ¼ cup (60 g) of the butter as needed.

Serve the *Kartoffelpuffer* with applesauce, sour cream or sprinkle them with sugar.

Oma's Ecke

Blender Potato Pancakes: When our children were little, I had a quick way to make these. I'd put 4 or 5 unpeeled new potatoes, 1 large egg, about ¼ cup (38 g) of chopped onions, ½ teaspoon of salt and 2 tablespoons (15 g) of flour in my blender. I'd pulse-blend the ingredients, scraping down the sides of the blender occasionally, until all the ingredients were mixed and little pieces of potatoes were left. (Going to the smoothie stage was a no-no, since I was trying to imitate the grated potato mixture.) Fried and served with sugar and applesauce, these were always a hit. Were they identical to the grated ones? No. But, that didn't matter. They were delicious and our family was fed and happy.

Schinkennudeln

(HAM AND NOODLES)

A child-friendly dish, these fried noodles were the perfect way for Oma to use up leftovers. With recollections of their childhood, many adults still consider this super easy dish to be their favorite comfort food.

Often, the cooked noodles or pasta were just fried in some butter with some ham, seasoned and served. Some liked pouring an egg and milk mixture over the almost finished dish and mixing it in until the eggs were cooked. Both versions are given here. In *Oma's Ecke,* I've added many more variations and changes that can be made. Use your imagination and include whatever things are lurking in your fridge that need to be used.

1 (16-oz [454-g]) package wide egg noodles (see *Oma's Ecke*)

2 tbsp (30 g) butter

1 cup (150 g) diced onions

½ lb (227 g) ham, cut into ½-inch (13-mm) cubes

Salt and freshly ground black pepper, as needed

2 tbsp (5 g) finely chopped fresh parsley, for garnish

4 large eggs, optional (see *Oma's Ecke*)

4 tbsp (60 ml) milk, optional

Cook the noodles according to the package instructions until they are al dente. Drain them and keep them warm.

Meanwhile, melt the butter in a large skillet over medium heat. Add the onions and sauté for 5 to 7 minutes, or until they are tender, stirring occasionally. Add the ham and sauté for 1 minute. Using a spatula, stir in the egg noodles and fry for 3 to 5 minutes, until the noodles are slightly crispy.

Season with salt and pepper. Garnish with the parsley and serve immediately.

If you want to add eggs, whisk the eggs and milk together in a small bowl. Pour this mixture over the noodles once they have been fried. Stir slowly for 2 to 3 minutes, until the eggs set. Season with salt and pepper. Garnish with the parsley and serve immediately.

Oma's Ecke

Schinkennudeln allows for many variations. Instead of egg noodles, use your favorite pasta. Omit the onions or double the amount. Add some leftover vegetables along with the ham. Don't have any ham? Use leftover meat, sausage or wieners. Stir in some grated cheese just before you add the eggs. Season with freshly grated nutmeg or your favorite herbs.

Instead of using eggs, make a sauce that you pour over the onion, ham and noodle mixture. Do this by melting 1 tablespoon (15 g) of butter in the skillet over medium heat. Whisk in 1 tablespoon (8 g) of flour until the roux is smooth, about 1 minute, but do not let it brown. Whisk in 1 cup (250 ml) of hot broth or cream and simmer for 5 minutes, stirring occasionally, until the sauce is smooth and thickened. Season with salt and pepper and pour over the noodle mixture.

Bremen

Though it is the smallest of the German states, Bremen packs a lot into a little space. Take the historical market square. The town hall (a UNESCO World Heritage site) was built in 1405 and boasts a 600-year-old statue of Roland, a symbol of freedom. On the other side of the square, by the state parliament building, there's a manhole cover where people stoop down to listen to the crowing, meowing, barking and hee-hawing of the Bremen Town Musicians, whose bronze sculpture stands not too far away. Under the town hall is the Ratskeller, a historical restaurant with its famous 1653 vintage cask rose wine. Though not on its menu, you'll find other wines and classic Bremen fare to enjoy.

Bremen's proximity to the North Sea and the Weser River has always provided easy access to foreign markets, which have greatly influenced the cooking for this region. Sweet, spicy and exotic. Curry, coffee and chocolate. A hodgepodge of cookery that is so satisfying. Try it. I think you'll like it!

Birnen, Bohnen und Speck

(PEARS, BEANS AND BACON)

Throughout the region, there are many variations for this typical northern dish. There are, however, certain established rules, such as "You must not cut off the pear stem," and "You must cut off the pear stem"; or, "You must not peel the pears," and "You must peel the pears." These rules mean that you really can create your own traditional recipe, just the way you like it. The main thing is that you must have the three main ingredients. Or, you can be like me and replace half or most of the bacon with some smoked sausage.

1¼ lb (570 g) smoked slab bacon or 4 smoked sausages

4 cups (1 L) cold beef broth

1 lb (454 g) fresh green beans, ends trimmed and broken in half

4 small firm pears with stems (see *Oma's Ecke*)

1 tsp dried summer savory

2 lbs (908 g) Yukon gold potatoes, peeled and quartered

Water, as needed

1 tsp salt

½ cup (75 g) chopped onions

2 tbsp (19 g) cornstarch mixed with 2 tbsp (30 ml) cold water

Salt and freshly ground black pepper, as needed

2 tbsp (5 g) finely chopped fresh parsley, for garnish

Cut the bacon into 5 pieces. Reserve 1 piece. If you are using sausages, pierce them with a fork.

Place 4 of the bacon pieces or the sausages in a large saucepan. Add the broth and bring it to a boil over high heat. Reduce the heat to medium-low and simmer for 10 minutes. Add the green beans, whole pears and summer savory. Simmer, covered, for 20 minutes.

Meanwhile, put the potatoes into another large saucepan and cover them with water. Add the salt and bring the potatoes to a boil over high heat. Cover the saucepan, reduce the heat to medium-low and simmer until the potatoes are tender, about 20 minutes. Drain the potatoes, put them back in the saucepan, cover the saucepan with a clean tea towel to absorb the steam and cover the towel with a lid to keep the potatoes warm.

While the bacon and potatoes are cooking, dice the reserved bacon. In a small skillet over medium heat, sauté the reserved bacon and onions for about 10 minutes, stirring occasionally, until the bacon fat is rendered and the onions are lightly caramelized. If you are using smoked sausages, sauté only the onions.

Just before serving, use a slotted spoon to transfer the pears, green beans and bacon from the saucepan to a large serving dish. Add just enough of the cornstarch slurry to the simmering cooking liquid to thicken the sauce, which will take about 2 minutes. Season it with salt and pepper. Pour some sauce over the green beans and put the rest of the sauce in a serving bowl to serve alongside. Sprinkle the sautéed bacon and onions over the green beans. Garnish with the parsley and serve with the potatoes.

Oma's Ecke

If you can't find the small cooking pears, you can use 2 Bosc pears. Cut them in half and remove the seeds using a melon baller. Do leave the peel on since it does look nice in the finished dish.

Grünkohl mit Pinkelwurst

(KALE WITH SAUSAGES)

Some would say that you can alter this recipe any way you like, but you *must* have *pinkelwurst* in it. However, if this smoked sausage isn't locally available, what can you do? You can still enjoy this classic Bremen dish. Just substitute your favorite smoked sausage—that's what you can do!

The same goes for the *kasseler*, another important German ingredient in this dish. It's a salt-cured and slightly smoked cut of pork loin. The closest to this and easiest to find would be a piece of ham. It definitely isn't the same, but close enough for this dish. If you want to be old-time traditional, change the first thirty minutes cooking time to two hours. Then refrigerate overnight and continue with the recipe the next day.

2 tbsp (30 g) clarified butter or 2 tbsp (30 ml) neutral oil

2 cups (300 g) diced onions

2 lbs (908 g) frozen kale (see *Oma's Ecke*)

⅓ lb (150 g) smoked slab bacon

1 dried bay leaf

2 cups (500 ml) beef broth

1 lb (454 g) *pinkelwurst* or smoked sausages

1 lb (454 g) *kasseler* or ham, thickly sliced

Water, as needed

Salt and freshly ground black pepper, as needed

Pinch of freshly grated nutmeg

Melt the butter in a large saucepan over medium heat. Add the onions and sauté for 5 minutes to soften them slightly. Add the kale, bacon and bay leaf. Pour in the broth, stir and reduce the heat to low. Cover the saucepan and simmer for about 30 minutes.

Poke the sausages several times with a fork. Place the sausages and *kasseler* on top of the kale and simmer, covered, over low heat for 30 minutes. Check the mixture occasionally to make sure there is liquid in the bottom of the saucepan. If needed, add a bit of water.

Transfer the bacon, *pinkelwurst* and *kasseler* to a serving dish. Cut the bacon into 4 pieces. Keep all the meat warm. Discard the bay leaf and season the kale with salt, pepper and nutmeg.

Serve the kale and meat with either boiled or pan-fried potatoes and good German mustard on the side.

Oma's Ecke

Kale tastes best when it's been harvested after being touched by frost. I recall my *mutti* planting kale, one of the few crops that would grow well in our northern Canadian climate. As a child, I wondered why Mutti didn't harvest the kale during the fall. Instead, she would go out in the winter, brush off the snow and cut it when she needed it. Now I know why. Kale that's been touched by frost is sweeter and more flavorful. That's why I prefer to buy mine right from the freezer section of my grocery store. No more waiting for winter.

Haschee

(GROUND BEEF SAUCE)

Often called *hackfleischsosse,* but sounding much more elegant as *haschee*, this ground beef sauce is usually served over mashed potatoes, noodles or rice. It really is a simple dish to make, a favorite among kids—and because of its simplicity, a favorite among cooks as well.

Although the traditional sauce is really just ground meat, adding vegetables helps extend the quantity deliciously. Mushrooms are a great addition but sliced green or red peppers would be wonderful too. Add a can of diced tomatoes or come up with your own additions. That's just how this *oma* makes it.

2 tbsp (30 g) clarified butter or
2 tbsp (30 ml) neutral oil

1 cup (150 g) diced onions

1½ lbs (680 g) lean ground beef

½ lb (227 g) button or cremini mushrooms, thickly sliced, optional

3 cups (750 ml) beef broth or water

1 tbsp (15 g) German whole-grain mustard

½ tsp paprika

Salt and freshly ground black pepper, as needed

1 tbsp (9 g) cornstarch mixed with 1 tbsp (15 ml) cold water

2 tbsp (5 g) finely chopped fresh parsley, for garnish

Melt the butter in a large skillet over medium heat. Add the onions and cook, stirring occasionally, for 5 to 7 minutes, or until the onions are tender but not browned. Add the ground beef and sauté, stirring frequently, until it is crumbly and lightly browned, about 5 minutes. Add the mushrooms (if using) and sauté for 1 minute. Pour in the broth and stir up any browned bits from the bottom of the skillet.

Reduce the heat to medium-low, bring the mixture to a simmer, cover the skillet and cook for 30 minutes. Depending on how much liquid evaporates, you may wish to add some extra broth or water.

Stir in the mustard and paprika. Season with salt and pepper. Stir in just enough of the cornstarch slurry to thicken the simmering sauce, which will take about 2 minutes. Add the parsley and serve.

Oma's Ecke

There are many ways to change this recipe by adding different herbs. Try adding 1 teaspoon dried thyme, oregano, basil or rosemary. Then, try a combination of them. You can also add 1 or 2 crushed cloves of garlic. A spoonful of tomato paste or some tomato juice are great as well. You can even change the meat to pork (or any combination).

Haschee comes from the French word *hachée*, and from there the German word, *hacken*, meaning, "to chop." That's exactly what this dish includes: chopped meats. Some aromatics and possibly veggies are added, a sauce is made and dinner is ready.

Kükenragout

(CHICK RAGOUT)

Yes, that's right. It's not chicken ragout, but chick ragout! Various tales abound about the origin of this dish—supposedly it contained not just little chicks, but calf's tongue and sweetbreads, crayfish and crabs, to mention just a few. Thankfully, nowadays, the ingredient list has become a whole lot tamer.

1 lb (454 g) boneless, skinless chicken breasts

2 cups (500 ml) chicken broth

½ lb (227 g) fresh green or white asparagus

3 tbsp (45 g) butter, divided

⅓ lb (150 g) small button mushrooms, halved

2 tbsp (16 g) all-purpose flour

1 tbsp (15 ml) fresh lemon juice

Salt and freshly ground black pepper, as needed

2 cups (300 g) frozen green peas, thawed

½ lb (227 g) small shrimp, peeled and deveined

1 tbsp (3 g) finely chopped fresh parsley, for garnish

Put the chicken breasts and the chicken broth into a medium saucepan over high heat. Bring to a boil, reduce the heat to low, cover the saucepan and simmer for 20 minutes, or until the chicken is tender. The internal temperature should be 165°F (74°C). Remove the chicken from the saucepan and set it aside until it is cool enough to handle. Cut the meat into bite-size pieces. Cover the saucepan so that the remaining broth will remain hot.

While the chicken is cooking, prepare the asparagus. If you are using green, just snap off the tough bottom portion of the stalk. If you are using white, peel it and cut off the tough bottom portion of the stalk. Bring a medium pot of water to a boil over high heat. Add the asparagus. Cook the green asparagus for 5 to 10 minutes and the white asparagus for 10 to 15 minutes. Take the asparagus out of the pot, shock it in a bowl of cold water, drain it and cut it into bite-size pieces.

Measure the remaining chicken broth from cooking the chicken. Add some asparagus cooking water, if needed, in order to have 2 cups (500 ml) of liquid.

Melt 1 tablespoon (15 g) of the butter in a large skillet over medium heat. Add the mushrooms and sauté until they are lightly browned, 5 to 8 minutes. Remove the mushrooms from the skillet and set them aside. Make a roux by melting the remaining 2 tablespoons (30 g) of the butter in the skillet. Whisk in the flour until the roux is smooth, about 1 minute, but do not let it brown. Whisk in the 2 cups (500 ml) of hot chicken broth. Bring the mixture to a boil, reduce the heat to low and simmer for 5 minutes, stirring occasionally, until the sauce is smooth and thickened.

Season the simmering sauce with the lemon juice and salt and pepper. Add the chicken, mushrooms, peas and shrimp. Stir and simmer for about 5 minutes, or until the shrimp have turned pink. Add the asparagus pieces and let them reheat in the sauce.

Serve the *Kükenragout* over rice and garnished with the parsley.

Oma's Ecke

The use of chicks in this may just be a word thing. It's now thought that *küken* actually refers to month-old chicks that are less than 1 pound (454 g) in weight, not newly hatched ones. These were also called *stubenküken*, which translates as "room chicks" since, in years past, these chicks were often kept in the house to protect them from the cold.

Brandenbur

Encircling Berlin, Brandenburg's landscape is a mix of 18,600 miles (30,000 km) of waterways and 3,000 lakes just waiting for your canoe, wakeboard or houseboat. You can also take a punt through the labyrinth of streams in the famous Spreewald Forest. If you'd rather stay on land, there are more than 4,000 miles (6,400 km) of cycle routes for you. You could even take an e-bike along the 160-mile (260-km) *Gurkenradweg* (Gherkin Cycle Path) and learn all about the renowned Spreewald gherkins.

The foods enjoyed by Brandenburgers, including those gherkins, have as much to do with its recent history as part of East Germany as it does with its landscape. Called Berlin's Vegetable Garden, this region is celebrated for its down-to-earth cooking, just like in *oma*'s kitchen, using what is locally grown and harvested.

Falscher Hase

(MEATLOAF)

As a child, I was glad my *mutti* cooked a *falscher hase* (false hare), because I could not imagine eating a real bunny. I never really knew what it was I was eating, other than it was really good. With the hard-boiled eggs hidden inside and covered with bacon, Mutti had a winner. It wasn't until I was older that I found out it was meatloaf, a classic food in many parts of the world.

Comfort food like this is what German cooking is all about. Extend this idea of nostalgia by having Bäckerkartoffeln (Scalloped Potatoes; page 117) on the side. Serve this at Easter and watch your children's eyes pop as you slice this at the table and they see the hidden eggs for the first time. (Adults' eyes open wide too!) If you wish, you can omit the hard-boiled eggs, but do not omit the bacon. The flavor it adds makes this meatloaf stand out from the ordinary.

6 large eggs, divided

1 tbsp (15 g) butter

1 cup (150 g) diced onions

1 stale kaiser roll, sliced (see *Oma's Ecke*)

¾ cup (175 ml) warm milk

2 lbs (908 g) lean ground beef or equal parts beef and pork

1½ tsp (8 g) salt

½ tsp freshly ground black pepper

½ tsp paprika

Breadcrumbs, if needed

6 slices bacon

Oma's Ecke

Using the soaked kaiser roll will produce a less dense meatloaf, a method used throughout Germany for almost any kind of meatloaf, hamburger or meatballs. If you do not have rolls to use, then bread will work as well, but avoid slices from a soft sandwich-style loaf. You can also replace this with ½ cup (60 g) of breadcrumbs.

Preheat the oven to 375°F (190°C). Grease the bottom of a large baking dish and set aside.

Place 3 of the eggs in a small pot and cover them with cold water. Bring the water to a boil over high heat and cook the eggs for 7 minutes. Drain the eggs and put them in a bowl of cold water to cool. Peel the cooled eggs and set them aside.

Melt the butter in a small skillet over medium heat. Add the onions and sauté, stirring occasionally, for 5 to 7 minutes, or until they are tender but not browned. Set the onions aside to cool.

Place the kaiser roll in a small bowl. Pour the milk over it and let it sit for 5 minutes. Drain the milk, squeeze the moisture out of the roll, crumble it and set aside.

To make the meatloaf, put the beef, the remaining 3 raw eggs, salt, pepper, paprika, sautéed onions and the crumbled kaiser roll into a large bowl. Mix the ingredients together with your hands. If the mixture is too moist to hold together, add some breadcrumbs.

Take half the meat mixture and form the bottom half of the loaf shape, about 9 x 4 inches (23 x 10 cm), down the middle of the baking dish. Lay the peeled hard-boiled eggs down the center and cover them with the remaining meat mixture. Gently press into a meatloaf shape.

Cover the meatloaf with the bacon strips and place the dish in the oven. Roast for 50 to 60 minutes, or until the meatloaf reaches an internal temperature of at least 165°F (74°C). Check in several places to make sure you are not just poking into the hidden eggs. Remove the meatloaf from the oven and let it stand for 10 minutes before slicing and serving.

Kartoffelsalat mit Mayo

(POTATO SALAD WITH MAYO)

There are as many traditional recipes for German potato salad as there are German *omas*. Each recipe has just a slight difference, meaning there isn't just one way of making it. There are, however, two main variations depending on which region in Germany you're from: southern Germans usually don't use mayonnaise and northerners do.

I must admit that this version of potato salad is my favorite, since it's the way I remember my *mutti* making it. Whenever I make it, I'm reminded of her and the little tips she'd give me as I helped her. For example, she'd tell me to cut the potatoes just thin enough that I could see the knife blade through them as I sliced.

2 lbs (908 g) red or Yukon gold potatoes, washed and unpeeled (see *Oma's Ecke*)

1 cup (220 g) mayonnaise

½ cup (125 ml) dill pickle brine

1 tsp salt, plus more as needed

½ tsp freshly ground black pepper, plus more as needed

½ cup (75 g) diced onions

3 medium dill pickles, diced

4 medium radishes, thinly sliced

4 large hard-boiled eggs, peeled and thinly sliced

1 tbsp (2 g) finely chopped fresh dill or chives

Oma's Ecke

I like using Yukon gold potatoes for my salads. They are considered an all-purpose potato and are great for almost any recipe. Other options include waxy potatoes, such as red potatoes, which have a low starch content. These hold together well after cooking. What you want to avoid are starchy potatoes, such as russets. However, if that's all you have available, you'll need to slice them thicker, so that they won't fall apart so easily when you're mixing the salad.

Put the potatoes in a large saucepan, cover them with cold water and bring them to a boil over high heat. Reduce the heat to medium-low and bring the water to a gentle boil. Cover the saucepan and cook until the potatoes are tender, 20 to 40 minutes, depending on their size. Check that the potatoes can be easily pierced with a knife, but do not overcook them. Drain the potatoes, let them cool, peel them and set them aside.

Make the dressing by whisking together the mayonnaise and pickle brine in a small bowl. In another small bowl, mix the salt and pepper. Place the onions, pickles, radishes and eggs each in a small bowl. Set the bowls in a row on a work surface to create an "assembly line."

Pour in a small amount of the dressing in a large bowl. Slice one-third of the potatoes into ⅛-inch (3-mm) slices and place over the dressing. Layer one-third of the onions, pickles, radishes and eggs over the potatoes. Sprinkle the top with some of the salt and pepper mix. Pour one-third of the dressing over the salt and pepper. Repeat these layers until all of the ingredients are used, finishing with as much of the remaining dressing as you think you need. This depends on the moisture content of the potatoes. You may want to start with a bit less and add more as the dressing soaks in.

Gently mix the salad using your hands. Season with more salt and pepper, if needed. Let the potato salad rest in the fridge for at least 1 hour for the flavors to mingle.

Serve garnished with the dill.

Kohlrouladen or Krautwickel

(CABBAGE ROLLS)

My *mutti* made the best cabbage rolls! They were the best because they had no rice and no tomato sauce. Just a wonderful, flavorful meat filling, nestled in browned cabbage and served with a delicious brown gravy. Additional seasonings can be added to the meat mixture, such as nutmeg, MAGGI® Liquid Seasoning, caraway seeds, paprika or thyme, making these cabbage rolls a versatile dish. Personally, I love adding Montreal steak seasoning, a totally non-German addition, but so good. It's pure comfort food, *oma*-style, especially when served with mashed potatoes.

1 (2-lb [908-g]) green or savoy cabbage

4 tsp (20 g) salt, divided, plus more as needed

4 tbsp (60 g) clarified butter or 4 tbsp (60 ml) neutral oil, divided

1 cup (150 g) diced onions

1 stale kaiser roll, sliced

¾ cup (175 ml) warm milk

¾ lb (340 g) lean ground beef

¾ lb (340 g) ground pork

2 large eggs

½ tsp freshly ground black pepper, plus more as needed

2 cups (500 ml) beef broth

2 tbsp (19 g) cornstarch mixed with 2 tbsp (30 ml) cold water

Set some wooden skewers or kitchen twine near your workspace for easy access.

To check the size of the pot needed, put the cabbage in a large pot and fill it with water so that the cabbage will be submerged. Remove the cabbage and add 3 teaspoons (15 g) of the salt to the water and bring to a boil over high heat. Fill a large bowl with cold water and set it aside.

Prepare the cabbage by removing any damaged outer leaves. Cut out the bottom core so that the leaves will loosen once they are boiled. Lower the cabbage carefully into the boiling water, with the bottom facing upward. Cook for 5 to 10 minutes, gently removing the leaves with tongs as they loosen from the core and placing them in the cold water to stop the cooking. Continue removing leaves until you have 8 large leaves. If they break or if the leaves are too small, remove extra leaves that you will layer together to create a larger leaf. Remove the rest of the cabbage from the boiling water and reserve it for another meal, such as cabbage soup.

Once the leaves are cold, remove them from the water. If any have thick veins, trim them thinner so that they will be easier to roll. Lay the leaves on a work surface and prepare the filling.

Melt 1 tablespoon (15 g) of the butter in a small skillet over medium heat. Add the onions and sauté, stirring occasionally, for 5 to 7 minutes, or until they are tender but not browned. Set the onions aside to cool.

Place the kaiser roll in a small bowl. Pour the milk over it and let it sit for 5 minutes. Drain the milk, squeeze the moisture from the roll, crumble it and set aside.

Place the beef, pork, eggs, onions, crumbled roll, the remaining 1 teaspoon of salt and the pepper in a large bowl. Gently mix with your hands. Divide the meat mixture into 8 portions and form each into an oval meatball. Place a meatball on the bottom end of each leaf. Roll the leaf up tightly, tucking in the sides, and fasten it with a skewer or wrap it with kitchen twine.

Melt the remaining 3 tablespoons (45 g) of the butter in a large saucepan over medium-high heat. In batches, brown the cabbage rolls on all sides, about 5 minutes. Set each batch of browned cabbage rolls aside as you brown the others. Return all the cabbage rolls to the saucepan and add the broth. Cover the saucepan and simmer over low heat for 1 hour. Transfer the cabbage rolls to a platter, removing the skewers or twine. Cover the platter to keep the rolls warm while you make the gravy.

Stir just enough of the cornstarch slurry into the simmering liquid to thicken the gravy, which will take about 2 minutes. Season with salt and pepper and serve the cabbage rolls with the gravy on the side.

Oma's Ecke

Want an easier way to prep the cabbage? Freeze the whole cabbage for a couple of days and thaw it in the fridge (which will take at least a day). Now, remove the leaves and use them. Not fast, but easy.

Pellkartoffeln, Quark und Leinöl

(POTATOES WITH QUARK AND FLAXSEED OIL)

Considered *arme-leute-essen* (poor people's food) because it is affordable and easy to make, this dinner is simplicity at its finest. With boiled potatoes, seasoned quark cheese and flaxseed oil on top, dinner's ready in no time at all.

I recall my *mutti* not having access to quark, and, not knowing how to make it herself, she'd take cottage cheese and press it through a sieve. With fresh chives from the garden, she would serve this when new potatoes were fresh at the market. Now, though, quark can be purchased outside of Germany in many places. If it is not available where you live, you can make your own, as shown in *Oma's Ecke*.

2 lbs (908 g) new potatoes, washed and unpeeled

1 tsp salt

2 cups (400 g) quark (see *Oma's Ecke*)

3 tbsp (45 ml) milk

4 tbsp (60 ml) fresh cold-pressed flaxseed oil, divided

2 green onions, finely chopped

½ cup (24 g) minced fresh chives, divided

Salt and freshly ground black pepper, as needed

3 tbsp (45 g) butter

Put the potatoes in a large saucepan, cover them with cold water, add the salt and bring the potatoes to a boil over high heat. Cover the saucepan, reduce the heat to medium-low and simmer until the potatoes are tender, about 20 minutes, depending on their size.

Meanwhile, whisk together the quark, milk and 1 tablespoon (15 ml) of the oil in a medium bowl until the mixture is creamy. Stir in the green onions and ¼ cup (12 g) of the chives. Season with salt and pepper. Set the quark mixture aside.

When the potatoes are tender (test them by poking them with the point of a knife), drain them and let them cool slightly. Peel the potatoes.

Divide the potatoes between the dinner plates, ladle a large scoop of quark beside them, drizzle the remaining 3 tablespoons (45 ml) of the oil over the quark, put a pat of butter by the potatoes and sprinkle the remaining ¼ cup (12 g) of the chives over everything.

Oma's Ecke

If you can't find quark in the store, you can easily make your own at home. Start by pouring 4 cups (1 L) of buttermilk into a Greek yogurt maker. Set it for a 12-hour incubation. Pour the incubated buttermilk into the accompanying sieve and let it drain in the fridge for 6 hours. The result? About 2 cups (400 g) of quark that can be used for the preceding dinner or to bake a fabulous German cheesecake. I use the leftover whey that drains off to make artisan bread.

Blumenkohl mit Semmelbrösel

(CAULIFLOWER WITH BUTTERED CRUMBS)

Whenever Mutti made cauliflower for dinner, I'd always ask for extra *semmelbrösel*. Why? Because these buttered crumbs made what could have been a ho-hum, mild vegetable absolutely extraordinary! In fact, she'd often include a small bowl of extra buttered crumbs on the table, just for us kids.

It's hard to believe that something so simple can make such a big difference. Adding these buttered crumbs to Brussels sprouts, green beans and other veggies makes them absolutely delicious. If you're willing to be totally different and creative with cauliflower, then you really also need to try the Blumenkohl-Bombe (Cauliflower Bomb with Mince and Bacon; page 170).

1 (2-lb [908-g]) cauliflower
(see *Oma's Ecke*)

1 tsp sugar

2¼ tsp (11 g) salt

1 cup (250 ml) milk

4 tbsp (60 g) butter

½ cup (60 g) breadcrumbs

You can either cook the cauliflower whole or separate it into florets.

If you are keeping it whole, trim the stalk end and cut an **X** into it. Place the cauliflower, stem-side down, in a large pot of boiling water to which you have added the sugar, 2 teaspoons (10 g) of the salt and milk. Reduce the heat to medium and simmer for 10 to 15 minutes, or until the cauliflower is just tender. Check by piercing it with the tip of a knife. If it goes in easily, it is done. Drain the cauliflower.

If you are cooking just the florets, add them to a large pot filled with about 3 inches (8 cm) of boiling water to which you have added the sugar, 2 teaspoons (10 g) of the salt and milk. Reduce the heat to medium and simmer the florets for 8 to 10 minutes, checking that they are just tender. Drain the florets.

Meanwhile, melt the butter in a small skillet over medium-high heat. Add the breadcrumbs and the remaining ¼ teaspoon salt. Fry the breadcrumbs, stirring, for 3 to 4 minutes, or until they are nicely browned. You will need to be careful that the crumbs do not burn. This can happen quickly. Remove the skillet from the heat and pour the breadcrumbs into a small bowl immediately so that they do not brown further.

Place the cauliflower in a serving dish and scatter the buttered crumbs over the top. Any extra crumbs can be served in a small bowl alongside.

Oma's Ecke

To help retain the cauliflower's white color, make sure you don't use an iron or aluminum pot. Another way to help keep it white is to add milk to the cooking water. The milk even sweetens it a bit.

Hessen

(Hesse)

Once upon a time, and through the centuries, the Celts, Chatti, ancient Romans, Saxons, Franks and Prussians all called this region home. A place where history, with its castles and knights, meets Sleeping Beauty's Sababurg Castle and the other fairy tales of the Brothers Grimm in the Reinhardswald Forest.

Located in the center of Germany, Hessen is almost half covered with woodlands. Perhaps that's why for centuries Frankfurt has celebrated *Wäldchestag* (Forest Day) with a modern version of a forest picnic, a fun fair with rides and food stalls of all types of gastronomy.

Dividing northern from southern Germany, Hessen's cuisine is a mix of both. There are some uniquely local dishes that are easy to make at home and that have today's Saxons, Franks and Prussians living happily ever after.

Hähnchen Cordon Bleu

(CHICKEN CORDON BLEU)

Cordon bleu always sounded very extravagant, very expensive, very French and very difficult to make, until I realized it was really nothing more than *rouladen* made with chicken breast. In other words, *hähnchen-rouladen*! The difficulty comes in butterflying the breasts and pounding them thin enough without making holes, so the stuffing won't leak out. However, there is an easier way. Just cut a pocket and stuff it: cordon bleu made in no time at all. Very extravagant, not expensive, not difficult and very German!

4 (6-oz [170-g]) boneless, skinless chicken breasts

Salt and freshly ground black pepper, as needed

4 slices Emmental or Gruyère cheese

4 slices deli-style Black Forest ham

1 cup (125 g) all-purpose flour

2 large eggs

2 tbsp (30 ml) milk

1 cup (120 g) seasoned breadcrumbs

Set some metal skewers near your workspace for easy access.

Prepare the chicken breasts by cutting them lengthwise horizontally into the thickest part of the breasts to create a pocket or flap. Sprinkle a little salt and pepper into the pocket as well as on the outside.

Put a slice of cheese on a slice of ham and roll it up tightly. Place it inside the chicken pocket. Use skewers to hold the pocket closed. Repeat this process until all the breasts are stuffed.

Set 3 shallow bowls on a work surface. Put the flour in one bowl. In the next bowl, beat together the eggs and milk. Put the breadcrumbs in the third bowl. Place a large plate nearby.

Dredge the chicken by taking one stuffed breast and rolling it first in the flour. Dip it in the egg mixture. Follow that by rolling it in the bread crumbs. Place it on the plate and repeat this process with the remaining chicken breasts, being careful that they don't touch each other on the plate. Place the plate in the fridge for at least 20 minutes. This will help the breading stick to the chicken. If you want to keep the breasts in the fridge for up to 1 day, cover them with plastic wrap.

Meanwhile, preheat the oven to 400°F (200°C). Lightly grease a large rimmed baking sheet. Place the chicken on the baking sheet. Bake for 25 to 30 minutes, or until the breasts reach an internal temperature of a least 160°F (71°C). Remove the chicken from the oven, take out the skewers and serve.

Oma's Ecke

Rolling something around something else to make something different—that's what *rouladen* are. For hundreds of years, *omas* in Germany have been making them from meats, fish and even cabbage.

Cordon bleu means "blue ribbon" in French, signifying a very high standard. At some point, these words were attached to schnitzel in Switzerland when veal was wrapped around cheese. Fast-forward to Germany, which already had *rouladen* and turned the *hähnchen-rouladen* into Hähnchen Cordon Bleu—that really does sound more exciting!

Bäckerkartoffeln

(SCALLOPED POTATOES)

Called *kartoffelgratin* elsewhere, these scalloped potatoes can be made two ways. The first one is messy and not always successful, and uses a flour-based sauce. The second is easy and uses heavy cream. I like easy and I like cream. Of course, the second way is German!

The preparation for this dish is easy, especially if you use a mandoline slicer to cut the potatoes. Heat the cream, pour it over the potatoes and pop them into the oven. *Ratze fatze*, or as one says in English: easy breezy. That's what makes this an ideal dish for company, because now you have about seventy-five minutes to do other things before the potatoes make an appearance at the table.

3 tbsp (45 g) butter, divided

1½ cups (375 ml) heavy cream

1 tsp salt

¼ tsp freshly ground black pepper

Pinch of freshly grated nutmeg

2½ lbs (1.1 kg) Yukon gold potatoes, peeled and cut into ⅛-inch (3-mm) thick slices

1 cup (120 g) grated Emmental cheese (see *Oma's Ecke*)

Preheat the oven to 360°F (182°C). Grease an 8 x 8-inch (20 x 20-cm) baking dish with 1 tablespoon (15 g) of the butter.

Combine the cream, salt, pepper and nutmeg in a small saucepan over medium-high heat. Bring the mixture to a boil, making sure it does not boil over. Reduce the heat to low and simmer for 1 minute.

Arrange the potato slices in the casserole dish. Pour the cream mixture over the potatoes.

Place the baking dish in the oven and bake for 60 minutes, or until the potatoes are easily pierced with the tip of a knife. Remove the potatoes from the oven.

Increase the oven temperature to 400°F (200°C). Sprinkle the cheese over the potatoes. Dot the remaining 2 tablespoons (30 g) of the butter over the top. Return the baking dish to the oven for 15 minutes, or until the top of the scalloped potatoes is golden brown and the cheese has melted.

Serve the potatoes hot.

If you'd like a bit more punch to this, fry 5 ounces (150 g) of diced air-dried, streaky smoked bacon in a bit of butter. Sprinkle that among the potato slices as you're arranging them in the baking dish.

Want even more punch? When you're frying the bacon, also fry up some sliced red onions and add them to the potatoes.

Still need more? Take a clove (or two or three) of garlic. Put it through a garlic press and rub it around the greased baking dish before you add the potatoes.

Emmental, the famous "Swiss Cheese" with all the holes, has a nutty, sweet and fruity taste. Can't find it? Then use your favorite melty cheese.

Schmandschnitzel

(SCHNITZEL WITH CREAM SAUCE)

There are so many variations to the simple schnitzel throughout Germany, with all kinds of wonderful sauces and seasonings. In Hessen, it's often served with *schmand*, a type of sour cream, flavored with fresh herbs, bacon, onions and leeks. It tastes as delightful as it sounds. Since *schmand* is rarely available outside of Germany, a good substitute for this recipe is full-fat sour cream.

CREAM SAUCE

1 tbsp (15 g) butter

3 oz (85 g) lean bacon, finely diced

½ cup (75 g) finely diced onions

1 large leek, white part only, sliced into thin rings

2 tbsp (5 g) finely chopped fresh parsley

2 tbsp (5 g) finely chopped fresh chives

2 tbsp (5 g) finely chopped fresh dill

½ tsp mild German mustard

1¾ cups (400 g) full-fat sour cream

Salt and freshly ground black pepper, as needed

SCHNITZEL

¾ cup (95 g) all-purpose flour

1 tsp salt

½ tsp freshly ground black pepper

½ tsp paprika

2 large eggs

2 tbsp (30 ml) milk

1½ cups (180 g) breadcrumbs

4 (5½-oz [155-g]) veal or pork schnitzel

4 tbsp (60 g) clarified butter or 4 tbsp (60 ml) neutral oil

2 tbsp (30 g) butter, divided

1 medium lemon, sliced, for garnish

To make the cream sauce, melt the butter in a medium saucepan over medium heat. Add the bacon and onions and cook, stirring occasionally, until the bacon fat is rendered and the onions are translucent, 5 to 7 minutes. Stir in the leek and fry 2 minutes. Remove the saucepan from the heat and stir in the parsley, chives and dill. Remove 2 tablespoons (23 g) of the mixture and set it aside. Add the mustard and sour cream to the saucepan. Stir and season with salt and pepper. Cover the saucepan and set it aside.

Preheat the oven to 160°F (71°C). Line a large baking sheet with parchment paper. Place several paper towels on a large plate. Have another large plate available. Set these aside.

To make the schnitzel, mix together the flour, salt, pepper and paprika in a shallow bowl. Mix together the eggs and milk in a second shallow bowl. Put the breadcrumbs in a third shallow bowl. Dredge 1 schnitzel in the flour, then in the eggs and then in the breadcrumbs. Place the schnitzel on the large unlined plate and repeat this process with the rest of the meat.

Melt the clarified butter in a large skillet over medium-high heat. Add 1 tablespoon (15 g) of the butter and when it has melted, add 1 or 2 schnitzel, making sure you do not crowd them. Cook until the schnitzel are golden brown on both sides, each side cooking for 3 to 4 minutes. Remove the schnitzel from the skillet and place them briefly on the plate lined with the paper towels and then on the prepared baking sheet in the oven. Cook the remaining schnitzel, adding the remaining 1 tablespoon (15 g) of butter.

Serve the schnitzel with the cooled cream sauce poured partially over the meat. Sprinkle the reserved bacon mixture over the top of the sauce and place a lemon slice on the side.

Oma's Ecke

Traditionally, schnitzels are to be swimming in the fat, but not deep-fried. There's a trick to getting the batter puffy on the schnitzel and that's to scoop some of the fat onto the sides and top of the schnitzel as it's frying. Not to submerge it, just to splash it on a bit. It's a technique worth trying.

Schweinepfeffer

(MARINATED SPICED PORK)

The translation for this is "peppered pork." Yet looking at the ingredient list, you'll find a normal amount of pepper. Historically, when a recipe was called "peppered," it meant it was well spiced. That's what this Schweinepfeffer is. There are two basic recipes for this: One omits the marinating stage; the other includes it. Me? I include it because it adds more flavor! All it requires is starting the meat a day or two before you want to serve it.

You'll notice that this is almost like goulash, so similar side dishes work: potato dumplings (Schneebällchen—Potato Dumplings from Cooked Potatoes; page 84) and red cabbage (Apfel-Rotkohl—Red Cabbage with Apples; page 184). Since this is pork, adding a bowl of applesauce will round out the meal.

2 lb (908 g) pork shoulder roast

3 cups (750 ml) red wine

2 tbsp (30 ml) red wine vinegar

1 large onion, coarsely chopped

2 dried bay leaves

4 black peppercorns

4 tbsp (60 g) butter

1 large onion, thickly sliced

2 cloves garlic, crushed

1 tsp dried marjoram

2 tbsp (19 g) cornstarch mixed with 2 tbsp (30 ml) cold water

Salt and freshly ground black pepper, as needed

Trim the pork of excess fat. Cut the roast into 1-inch (2.5-cm) slices. Put them into a resealable freezer bag. You can also use a glass or ceramic bowl that is just big enough for the meat and marinade. Add the red wine, vinegar, chopped onion, bay leaves and peppercorns. Seal the bag. If you are using a bowl, cover it with plastic wrap. Place the meat in the fridge for 8 to 48 hours, turning the meat several times during that time.

Remove the meat from the marinade. Dry it well with paper towels and cut the slices into 1-inch (2.5-cm) cubes. Strain the marinade through a sieve and set it aside.

Melt the butter in a large saucepan over medium-high heat. Add the pork cubes in batches and brown them on all sides, 5 to 8 minutes. Transfer the meat to a large bowl and add the sliced onion to the saucepan. Reduce the heat to medium and sauté for 8 to 10 minutes, or until the onion is golden brown. Add the strained marinade, stirring to loosen up any browned bits at the bottom of the saucepan. Return the meat to the saucepan, adding the garlic and marjoram. Reduce the heat to medium-low, bring the mixture to a simmer, cover the saucepan and cook for 45 to 60 minutes, until the pork is tender.

Stir just enough of the cornstarch slurry into the simmering liquid to thicken the gravy, which should take about 2 minutes. Season with salt and pepper and serve.

Oma's Ecke

You may wonder why I slice the meat before I marinate it. It could be done in one piece, but it would need to marinate longer. Sliced, it goes quicker. However, if it were already cut into cubes and then marinated, it would certainly go even faster. But you'd have to pick through the cubes to pull out the spices and the bits of onion before you brown them. Not much fun.

Frankfurter Grüne Sosse

(FRANKFURT'S GREEN SAUCE)

Wander through the markets in Hessen in the springtime, particularly in the Frankfurt area, and you will see strange bundles wrapped in white paper and labeled *grüne sosse*. Within these bundles are the seven required herbs for this special sauce: parsley, chives, chervil, borage, sorrel, garden cress and burnet. If these herbs are not available where you live, then substitute with some tarragon, dill, summer savory, lovage or lemon balm. Alternatively, you could just use several of your favorites, such as parsley, chives, watercress and sorrel.

Called *frankfurter grie soss* in the dialect of the area, this cold sauce is served with boiled potatoes and hard-boiled eggs. Since the herbs are available in the springtime, this is also served on Maundy Thursday (the Thursday before Easter), which in German is *Gründonnerstag* (literally "Green Thursday"), making this green sauce a perfect choice.

10 oz (280 g) fresh herbs (see recipe headnote)

4 large hard-boiled eggs, peeled and cut in half

2 green onions, finely chopped

1 tbsp (15 ml) white wine vinegar

2 cups (460 g) sour cream

1 cup (230 g) Greek yogurt (see *Oma's Ecke*)

1 tbsp (15 g) whole-grain mustard, optional

2 tbsp (30 ml) sunflower oil, optional

Pinch of sugar

Salt and freshly ground black pepper, as needed

Wash the fresh herbs thoroughly. Dry them either in a salad spinner or with paper towels. Cut off any thick stems.

Separate the yolks from the eggs. Dice the whites very finely and set them aside.

Place all the herbs, egg yolks, green onions, vinegar, sour cream, yogurt, mustard and oil (if using) in a food processor. Pulse until the herbs are pureed and the sauce is green and smooth. If a food processor is not available, chop the herbs very finely, place them in a medium bowl and stir well with the other ingredients.

Season the sauce with the sugar, salt and pepper. Place the sauce in a medium bowl, cover the bowl and refrigerate for at least 1 hour. Stir in the egg whites and season with additional salt and pepper, if needed, before serving.

Oma's Ecke

A similarity with the Italian *salsa verde* may be evident, since the origins of Frankfurt's sauce seems to come from there. The similarity ends with the herbs. Instead of vinegar and olive oil, Germans decided that cream was necessary. Originally made with mayonnaise, this has changed over the years. Now, various combinations of quark, crème fraîche, sour cream, Greek yogurt and buttermilk, all full-fat, are used for this very German sauce.

Schleswig Holstein

"Moin, moin!" That's the greeting you'll get when you visit this most northern German state, a place where Vikings, knights and pilgrims once roamed. Located between the stormy North Sea with its harsh climate and the relatively calm Baltic Sea, you'll find inland forests, moors and hills—perfect places to hike, bike and relax.

Cycle from the Wadden Sea with its tidal flats along the North Sea to the cliffs of the *Ostseeküste* (Baltic coast). Pedal alongside the Kiel Canal and arrive just in time for *Kieler Woche* (Kiel Week), the world's largest sailing event. Join millions of other people not only to see the thousands of ships, but also to enjoy the music and indulge in foreign and local food specialties at this annual *volksfest* (festival).

Produce from the sea and the land is abundant here. It's the basis for hearty dishes that are found throughout the region, whether in a gourmet spot or a cozy *gasthaus* (restaurant). This region is full of delicious food that is easy to make at home.

Bauerntopf

("FARMER'S POT"—GROUND BEEF STEW)

In years gone by, *burenpott*, as this recipe is called in the dialect of Schleswig-Holstein, would be made in one pot and pushed to the back of the woodstove to slowly simmer while the farm chores were being done. When it was time to eat, dinner was ready. Today, this kind of *eintopf* (one-pot meal), is still a traditional meal throughout Germany.

1 tbsp (15 g) clarified butter or 1 tbsp (15 ml) neutral oil

3 oz (85 g) lean bacon, finely diced

1¼ lbs (570 g) lean ground beef

1 cup (150 g) diced onions

2 cloves garlic, thinly sliced

2 tbsp (32 g) tomato paste

1½ cups (375 ml) vegetable or beef broth

1½ lbs (680 g) peeled Yukon gold potatoes, cut into ¾-inch (2-cm) cubes

8 oz (227 g) carrots, cut into ½-inch (13-mm) cubes

1 large green bell pepper, cut into ¾-inch (2-cm) pieces

1 large yellow, red or orange bell pepper, cut into ¾-inch (2-cm) pieces

1 (28-oz [800-g]) can diced tomatoes, undrained

½ tsp salt, plus more as needed

¼ tsp freshly ground black pepper, plus more as needed

1 tsp dried marjoram

1 tsp caraway seeds

1 tbsp (6 g) hot or sweet paprika

1½ cups (345 g) sour cream, divided

Finely chopped fresh chives or parsley, for garnish

Combine the butter and bacon in a large saucepan over medium-high heat. Sauté until the bacon fat has rendered, about 5 minutes. Add the ground beef and sauté, stirring frequently, for 5 to 8 minutes, until it is crumbly and lightly browned. Stir in the onions, garlic and tomato paste. Sauté for 5 minutes. Stir in the broth and scrape up any browned bits at the bottom of the saucepan. Add the potatoes, carrots, green bell pepper, yellow bell pepper, diced tomatoes, salt and pepper. Stir to combine.

Reduce the heat to medium-low, bring the mixture to a simmer, cover the saucepan and cook for 40 minutes. Remove the saucepan's lid and cook for 10 minutes to reduce the liquid. Add the marjoram, caraway seeds and paprika. Season with salt and pepper.

Remove the saucepan from the heat and stir in 1 cup (230 g) of the sour cream. Serve in soup bowls with a dollop of the remaining ½ cup (115 g) of the sour cream and sprinkled with the chives.

Oma's Ecke

This recipe allows for lots of variations. Change the veggies to include your favorites or to use up whatever your fridge is overflowing with. Change the spices by omitting the marjoram and caraway seeds and including other favorites. I like to add Montreal steak seasoning, a totally non-German addition that adds a nice kick to the dish. The traditional ground beef can easily be interchanged with pork or chicken. A combination of meats would also work well. Adding a sliced smoked sausage or two will give you some added zing. Turn Oma's *Bauerntopf* into your own creation!

Gestovte Kartoffeln

(CREAMED POTATOES)

For the Schleswig-Holsteiners, *gestovte* implies a sauce made with butter and flour. This recipe, however, uses cream—and not just plain cream, but heavy cream! There's no need for flour to thicken the potatoes, since they provide their own starch, making this a really easy dish to prepare. It's a perfect accompaniment for a simple meal of sausage, hamburgers or schnitzel. Actually, it's perfect for any meat that doesn't have gravy, since the cream in this one is rich enough.

1¾ lbs (800 g) red or Yukon gold potatoes (see *Oma's Ecke*)

1¼ cups (300 ml) heavy cream

3 tbsp (8 g) finely chopped fresh parsley or chives

Salt and freshly ground black pepper, as needed

Freshly grated nutmeg, optional

Put the potatoes in a large saucepan, cover them with water and bring them to a boil over high heat. Reduce the heat to medium-low, cover the saucepan and simmer until the potatoes are just tender, 25 to 30 minutes, depending on their size. Do not overcook the potatoes. Drain and cool the potatoes slightly under cold running water.

Once they are just cool enough to handle, peel the potatoes and cut them into ½-inch (13-mm) thick slices. Put the slices into the saucepan and add the cream. Place the saucepan over medium heat and bring the cream to a simmer, stirring gently to keep it from settling on the bottom and burning. While you're stirring, the starch from the potatoes is released and mixes with the cream, making a wonderfully creamy sauce. This will take about 10 to 15 minutes. Once the sauce is thick enough, remove the saucepan from the heat and stir in the chopped parsley.

Season the potatoes with salt and pepper and nutmeg (if using). Pour the potatoes into a serving dish and serve.

Oma's Ecke

It's important that you do not use starchy potatoes, such as russets. They'll fall apart during the cooking process and you will end up with mashed potatoes. That's not the texture you want here!

Cooking potatoes in their skins is very common in Germany. The name for these are *pellkartoffeln.* When cooking them this way, try to find similarly sized and shaped potatoes, not too small or too big. That way, they become tender at the same time.

I recall, as a child, stabbing the cooked potatoes with a fork to hold, because they were still too hot for me. It was easy for me to peel them that way. When a smaller potato came my way, as soon as I peeled it, I'd pop it into my mouth. I loved potatoes then, and I love them now. That's probably why this recipe appeals to me. That . . . and the cream.

Putensteaks mit Erbsen und Wurzeln

(TURKEY WITH PEAS AND CARROTS)

The *wurzeln* that accompany this very traditional veggie combo literally translate as "roots." In the north, this means carrots. Known as *karotten, möhren, mohrrüben* and *rüben* throughout the rest of Germany, they are usually served with peas as a quick and easy side to almost any meal. Here they're served with turkey, which is more popular sold as schnitzel or steaks than a whole bird. Just a quick fry of the steaks and dinner is ready in almost no time at all, perfect when you've had a busy day yet want something homemade. These *putensteaks* are also delicious together with Gestovte Kartoffeln (Creamed Potatoes; page 129), since they have their own creamy sauce.

PEAS AND CARROTS

4 cups (560 g) frozen peas and carrots (see *Oma's Ecke*)

3 tbsp (45 g) butter

Sugar, salt and freshly ground black pepper, as needed

2 tbsp (5 g) finely chopped fresh parsley

TURKEY

4 (6-oz [170-g]) turkey steaks

Salt and freshly ground black pepper, as needed

Pinch of cayenne pepper or paprika, optional

2 tbsp (30 g) clarified butter or 2 tbsp (30 ml) neutral oil

3 tbsp (45 g) butter, optional

To make the peas and carrots, cook the frozen peas and carrots according to the package instructions or until just tender. Drain the peas and carrots and transfer them to a medium pot over medium heat. Stir in the butter until it is melted. Remove from the heat. Season the peas and carrots with the sugar, salt and pepper. Add the parsley, cover and keep warm until ready to serve.

To make the turkey, pound the turkey steaks between two sheets of plastic wrap until they are no more than ½-inch (13-mm) thick. Sprinkle each side with salt, pepper and cayenne (if using). Melt the clarified butter in a large skillet over medium-high heat and add the turkey steaks. Sauté each side for about 4 minutes. The internal temperature should be at least 165°F (74°C). Transfer the turkey steaks to a serving dish.

If you would like some pan juices to pour over the turkey, melt the butter in the same skillet over medium-high heat, stirring up any browned bits. Keep stirring until the butter starts to brown, 2 to 3 minutes. Pour this over the turkey just before serving with the peas and carrots on the side.

Oma's Ecke

If you're in a hurry, you can use canned veggies instead. My *mutti* always had cans of peas and carrots available. She'd make a flour and butter roux to thicken the drained liquid from the can and add the veggies to heat through. That way they were done in a matter of minutes. I like using frozen veggies, especially a mix of peas, carrots and corn, but I do not let them get as mushy as Mutti did. I do like them with just a bit of bite. Healthier, too.

Lübecker Schwalbennester

("SWALLOWS' NESTS"—CHICKEN OR VEAL ROLLS)

Swallows' nests are an expensive delicacy in China, where these real nests contain solidified bird saliva and are prized for their unusual flavor. Here in Lübeck, they look more like Scottish eggs and, thankfully, have nothing to do with the real thing!

Lübecker schwalbennester are hard-boiled eggs that are wrapped in either veal or chicken along with ham and sometimes cheese. Served with a delicious gravy, these easy-to-make rolled treats are fun for kids and adults alike. Serve them cut in half to show off their unusual insides or keep it a surprise and serve them whole. They are delicious served with a side of boiled or mashed potatoes, spring vegetables or salad.

4 (5½-oz [155-g]) chicken or veal cutlets

Salt and freshly ground black pepper, as needed

4 thin slices deli-style ham

4 medium hard-boiled eggs, peeled

⅓ cup (42 g) all-purpose flour

2 tbsp (30 g) clarified butter or 2 tbsp (30 ml) neutral oil

2 cups (500 ml) hot chicken or beef broth, white wine or water

2 tbsp (19 g) cornstarch mixed with 2 tbsp (30 ml) cold water

2 tbsp (30 g) sour cream

Set some metal skewers or kitchen twine near your workspace for easy access.

Gently pound each chicken cutlet between two sheets of plastic wrap until it is very thin, being careful not to rip holes in the meat.

Sprinkle each cutlet with a little salt and pepper. Place 1 slice of ham and 1 egg on each cutlet. Roll the cutlet up to encase the egg and fasten the meat with kitchen twine or skewers. Put the flour in a shallow bowl and roll each nest in the flour. Shake off the excess flour.

Melt the butter in a large skillet over medium heat. Add the swallows' nests and fry for 5 to 7 minutes, turning the nests frequently so that all sides are browned evenly. Add the broth and scrape up any browned bits. Bring the broth to a simmer, reduce the heat to medium-low, cover the skillet and cook for 30 minutes.

Place the nests on a serving plate, removing the twine or skewers. Cover them to keep them warm while you make the gravy. Add just enough of the cornstarch slurry to the simmering liquid in the skillet to thicken the gravy, which will take about 2 minutes. Remove the skillet from the heat and stir in the sour cream. Season with salt and pepper. Serve with the gravy on the side.

Oma's Ecke

Although this recipe comes from northern Germany, it would be absolutely delicious served with a southern side dish: Spätzle (Homemade Egg Noodles; page 60). It's fun mixing cuisines from the different regions and coming up with your own special combination. For a more southern recipe for *schwalbennester*, there's one that uses ground meat to encircle the egg, more similar to the Scottish egg. It's known as the *Sauerländer Schwalbennester*, with Sauerland being the southeast part of North Rhine-Westphalia.

Gestovte Bohnen

(CREAMED GREEN BEANS)

It was so common to go into Oma's kitchen and find jars and jars of green beans from her garden filling the pantry. Turning these into absolute deliciousness required only a few extra ingredients, which were readily available (especially on the farm): herbs, butter and cream. The word *gestovte* is a *plattdeutsch* (low German dialect) word meaning "the dish has a sauce made with butter and flour."

The beans were often called *schnippelbohnen* (snipped beans), indicating that they were cut in very small pieces. In fact, one can still buy a *bohnen-schneider* (bean-cutting machine) just like Oma used. This allowed older and tougher beans to be used and still become tender in cooking. Today, frozen beans replace the home-jarred ones, but there's not much that can replace the richness that the cream provides.

Boiling water, as needed

1 tsp salt, plus more as needed

1½ lbs (680 g) frozen green beans

3 tbsp (45 g) butter

3 tbsp (24 g) all-purpose flour

1 cup (250 ml) heavy cream
(see *Oma's Ecke*)

1 cup (250 ml) milk, or as needed

Pinch of sugar

Freshly ground black pepper, as needed

1 tsp dried summer savory

4 tbsp (10 g) finely chopped fresh parsley, divided

In a medium saucepan, bring 1 inch (2.5 cm) of water to a boil over medium-high heat. Add the salt and the green beans. Cover and cook until the beans are tender, about 3 to 6 minutes. Drain the green beans and put them in a medium bowl.

Melt the butter in the same saucepan over medium heat. Whisk in the flour and continue stirring until the roux is smooth, about 1 minute, but do not let it brown. Whisk in the cream until the sauce is smooth, adding as much milk as is necessary to get to a creamy, thick sauce. Simmer for 5 minutes, stirring occasionally. Season the sauce with the sugar, salt, pepper and summer savory. Add 2 tablespoons (5 g) of the parsley. Gently stir in the green beans and reheat them for 1 minute in the sauce.

Serve the Gestovte Bohnen garnished with the remaining 2 tablespoons (5 g) of the parsley.

Oma's Ecke

Instead of using cream, you can replace this with all milk, vegetable broth or the water that the beans were cooked in. Freshly grated nutmeg is a nice addition either with or instead of the summer savory. To add even more flavor, fry some diced smoked ham in a bit of butter and add that to the finished beans.

This sauce is used throughout this area for other vegetables as well. Peas and carrots, kale, turnips, potatoes, lentils, cabbage and mixed vegetables are just a few options. Try your own combinations and see what your favorites are.

Saarland

France, Luxembourg and Germany come together in Saarland, one of the smallest states. You can experience cultures that go back two thousand years. Start with the excavated and reconstructed Roman Villa Borg in Perl. Move on to one of the largest Celtic fortresses in Europe, the "Ring of the Huns" in Otzenhausen. Then, follow the Baroque Road that takes you to the seventeenth- and eighteenth-century castles and imperial residences.

Under the ruins of the Hohenburg Castle, you can meander through the largest man-made mottled sandstone caves in Europe. Follow that with a tour through the beautiful river valleys, peaceful villages, forests and vineyards.

And then there's the food. Known for its many top chefs, food connoisseurs and Michelin stars, the dishes often have a touch of French cuisine with very local influences, such as Dibbelabbes (Potato Hash with Leeks; page 142)— gourmet and rustic at the same time. Except for the Villa Borg. There, they still cook from the original recipes written by the Roman gourmet Apicius from the first century AD.

Schnitzel mit Champignon-Sosse

(SCHNITZEL WITH MUSHROOM SAUCE)

There are three basic types of *schnitzel* in Germany: plain, breaded and rolled. These are usually made from four meats: veal, pork, chicken and turkey. Combining these possibilities with the most common sauces, gravies and fillings means that you could enjoy schnitzel every night of the week for a month without repeating a dish.

There are some meals that an *oma* would make that could take hours to prepare. Other times, she wanted something really quick and simple. This is one of those. Just pure schnitzel, served with a simple mushroom sauce. No breading. No wine. No bacon. Just simple, traditional flavors that come together in almost no time at all.

5 tbsp (75 g) clarified butter or 5 tbsp (75 ml) neutral oil, divided

4 (5½-oz [155-g]) pork schnitzel

Salt and freshly ground black pepper, as needed

1 cup (150 g) diced onions

1 lb (454 g) mushrooms, thinly sliced (see *Oma's Ecke*)

1 cup (250 ml) vegetable or beef broth

½ cup (125 ml) heavy cream

2 tbsp (5 g) finely chopped fresh parsley

Melt 2 tablespoons (30 g) of the butter in a large skillet over medium-high heat. Add the schnitzel, making sure you do not crowd them. (You may need to cook them in batches.) Fry them for 3 to 4 minutes on each side, or until each side is browned and the schnitzel is cooked through. Transfer the schnitzel to a plate. Season both sides with salt and pepper. Cover them to keep them warm.

Melt the remaining 3 tablespoons (45 g) of the butter in the same skillet over medium heat. Add the onions and sauté until they are translucent, 5 to 7 minutes. Add the mushrooms and sauté for 2 to 3 minutes. Stir in the broth, loosening any browned bits from the bottom of the skillet. Reduce the heat to medium-low and simmer, uncovered, for 10 minutes. Stir in the cream and the parsley. If the sauce is too thin, let it simmer for a few minutes to reduce. Season with salt and pepper. Add the schnitzel to warm them through.

Serve with Bratkartoffeln (Fried Potatoes; page 26) or Spätzle (Homemade Egg Noodles; page 60) and a green salad on the side.

Oma's Ecke

When you look at German recipes, you'll find there are two words used for mushrooms: *pilze* and *champignons,* with the latter used more frequently. The word has flair, sounding like some special French cuisine, which is so perfect for this Saarland region. When my *mutti* used it, I always thought we were having something extraordinary. In reality, they're a variety of mushroom, so that all *champignons* are *pilze,* but not all *pilze* are *champignons.* If you have champignon mushrooms available, do use them. If not, use whatever type is your favorite. Where I live, I can often find button mushrooms and creminis, both of which work fine for this recipe. If you have other favorites available, try them here as well.

Schweineschmorbraten

(BRAISED PORK ROAST)

Braising always produces a wonderfully moist meat with a rich gravy. And when you're using a pork butt or shoulder roast, the resulting meal is not only economical but also a truly scrumptious feast. Add to the meat some potato dumplings (Schneebällchen—Potato Dumplings from Cooked Potatoes; page 84) or bread dumplings (Semmelknödel—Bread Dumplings; page 59) and red cabbage (Apfel-Rotkohl—Red Cabbage with Apples; page 184). Of course, sauerkraut and applesauce would be perfect as well. This is a delectable family meal that both the guests and the cook will appreciate, since the meat is quite easy to prepare.

3 tbsp (45 g) clarified butter or
3 tbsp (45 ml) neutral oil

2 lb (908 g) boneless pork butt or
shoulder roast

2 large carrots, thickly sliced

1 large leek, thickly sliced

1 cup (227 g) cubed celeriac or 1 cup
(100 g) coarsely chopped celery

2 large onions, diced

2 cups (500 ml) beef broth, plus
more as needed

1 tsp salt, plus more as needed

1 tsp paprika

½ tsp freshly ground black pepper,
plus more as needed

2 tbsp (19 g) cornstarch mixed
with 2 tbsp (30 ml) cold water
(see *Oma's Ecke*)

Melt the butter in a large saucepan over medium-high heat. Brown the pork roast well on all sides for 8 to 10 minutes. Transfer the roast to a plate and add the carrots, leek, celeriac and onions to the saucepan and sauté for 3 to 5 minutes. Add the broth and scrape up any browned bits from the bottom of the saucepan. Sprinkle the salt, paprika and pepper over the roast. Return the roast to the saucepan. Cover the saucepan, reduce the heat to medium-low and simmer for 1½ to 2 hours, or until the meat is tender, turning the roast once after the first half hour.

Transfer the roast to a serving platter, cover it and let it rest for 10 minutes before serving.

In the meantime, strain the cooking liquid through a sieve into a large bowl, pressing on the vegetables to extract as much liquid as possible. Pour the strained cooking liquid back into the saucepan, adding more broth if more gravy is desired. Bring the cooking liquid to a simmer over medium-high heat and stir in just enough of the cornstarch slurry to thicken the gravy (which will take about 2 minutes). Season the gravy with salt and pepper.

Slice the meat against the grain and serve with the gravy on the side.

Oma's Ecke

If you wish, you can use an immersion blender instead of straining the cooking liquid. That way, all the goodness of the vegetables remains as part of the gravy. Thickening the gravy with the cornstarch will probably not be necessary in this case. Including the vegetables will mean that the flavor of the gravy will be slightly different than if they are strained out. The texture will not be quite as silky, but it still tastes really good—and it may just be a sneaky way to get non–veggie lovers to eat some extra veggies.

Dibbelabbes

(POTATO HASH WITH LEEKS)

There are two similar recipes, *dibbelabbes* and *schales*, that are popular in Saarland. I've taken the best of both to make a crust-filled potato hash for potato lovers everywhere. Served with the traditional side of homemade applesauce and an endive salad, it's a meal to make every *oma* proud.

When I say "crust-filled," that's exactly what I mean. Normally, a crust is on the top or the bottom of a dish. In *dibbelabbes*, the crust is created in the bottom of the pan-fried potato hash. As soon as a wonderful crust is formed, it gets stirred up so that more crust can form. Those crusty bits soon fill the whole hash and are the crowning feature of this potato dish.

3 lbs (1.4 kg) peeled waxy potatoes (such as red potatoes)

4 tbsp (60 g) clarified butter or 4 tbsp (60 ml) neutral oil, divided

½ lb (227 g) lean slab bacon, cut into ¼-inch (6-mm) cubes

2 medium leeks, cut into ¼-inch (6-mm) slices

1 large egg

Salt and freshly ground black pepper, as needed

Freshly grated nutmeg, as needed

2 tbsp (5 g) finely chopped fresh parsley, for garnish

Grate the potatoes and put them in a sieve over a bowl. Press down on the potatoes to remove as much water as possible. Let them drain for 10 to 15 minutes, pressing down occasionally.

Meanwhile, in a large skillet over medium heat, melt 2 tablespoons (30 g) of the butter. Add the bacon and sauté until most of the fat has been rendered, about 5 minutes. Add the leeks and sauté for 1 to 2 minutes to soften them. Remove the skillet from the heat and set aside to cool.

Carefully pour the liquid out of the bowl that is sitting under the potatoes, keeping the starch that has settled on the bottom of the bowl. Scrape up the starch, then add the grated potatoes and egg. Mix everything together using your hands. When the ingredients are thoroughly combined, mix in the bacon and leek mixture.

Heat the same skillet over medium heat. Add the potato hash and fry for about 5 minutes, until a golden-brown crust develops on the bottom. Using a spatula, scrape the crust up by turning over the potatoes, break the crust into pieces and let a new crust develop. Continue this crust building process, adding the remaining 2 tablespoons (30 g) of the butter if necessary, and regulating the heat so that this is a fairly slow process to allow the potatoes time to cook through. This whole process will take around 20 minutes. During this time, season the hash with salt, pepper and nutmeg.

The resulting potato hash will be filled with crusty bits throughout. Serve this hot from the skillet, garnished with the parsley and with a bowl of applesauce on the side.

Oma's Ecke

Dibbelabbes can be baked just like Döppekooche (Potato Casserole with Bacon; page 83) and, actually, the recipes appear very similar. In order to get the crustiness, you would need to stir the potatoes at least once during the baking process in order to break up the top crust and provide more surface for more crust to form.

Saarländische Mehlknepp

(FLOUR DUMPLINGS WITH CREAM SAUCE)

What does an *oma* do when the cupboards are almost bare? She makes *mehlknepp* if she lives in Saarland. With the barest of ingredients, she prepares the *geschiedene* (divorced) version if the dumplings are served alone, but when mixed with potatoes, they are the *verheiratete* (married) version. Covered with a bacon cream sauce, this dumpling and potato mixture becomes comfort food that's easy and quick to prepare.

1½ lbs (680 g) peeled Yukon gold potatoes, quartered lengthwise

3 tsp (15 g) salt, divided, plus more as needed

1 tbsp (15 g) clarified butter or 1 tbsp (15 ml) neutral oil

½ lb (227 g) lean slab bacon, diced

¾ cup (175 ml) heavy cream

¾ cup (175 ml) milk

Freshly ground black pepper, as needed

3⅔ cups (450 g) all-purpose flour (see *Oma's Ecke*)

4 large eggs

1 cup (250 ml) water, plus more as needed

Pinch of freshly grated nutmeg

Put the potatoes in a medium saucepan, cover them with water, add 1 teaspoon of the salt and bring the potatoes to a boil over high heat. Cover the saucepan, reduce the heat to medium-low and simmer until the potatoes are tender, about 20 minutes. Drain them when they are done, cover the saucepan with a clean tea towel to absorb the steam and cover the towel with the saucepan's lid to keep the potatoes warm.

Meanwhile, melt the butter in a medium skillet over medium heat. Add the bacon and fry until the fat is rendered, about 5 minutes. Pour in the cream and milk, stir and bring the mixture to a simmer for about 2 minutes, until it is slightly thickened. Season the sauce with additional salt (if needed) and pepper. Cover the skillet and set it aside to keep the sauce warm.

Bring a large pot of water to a simmer over high heat and add 1 teaspoon of the salt. Reduce the heat to medium-low to maintain a gentle simmer.

In a large bowl, combine the flour, eggs, the 1 cup (250 ml) of water, the remaining 1 teaspoon of salt and nutmeg. Mix the ingredients well into a thick yet fluid dough. Add more water, if needed. Using a spoon dipped in water, drop spoonfuls of the dough into the simmering water, dipping the spoon in water again before making each dumpling. Simmer the dumplings for 5 to 8 minutes after they rise to the top. Remove them with a slotted spoon and put them in a large serving dish.

Add the cooked potatoes to the dumplings. Pour the sauce over the dumplings and potatoes. Serve with a salad or a bowl of homemade applesauce on the side.

Oma's Ecke

Since the moisture content of flour changes with the seasons, getting the dough to the right consistency is a learned skill. Practice, and you'll soon be able to throw together this quick and easy dish. You may even want to add some onions to the bacon as you fry it and let them caramelize. They make for a really nice addition.

Lachsen

(Saxony)

Called the cultural capital of Germany and Germany's bakery, Saxony has much to offer. Climb aboard one of the oldest paddle steamers in the world for a trip down the Elbe River. Its stunning landscape is beset with castles and baroque buildings that will make you want to disembark to visit the Zwinger Palace or to take a walk along the Augustusstrasse to see one of the world's largest ceramic murals made from twenty-three thousand Meissen tiles.

Travel along the Leipzig Music Trail—think Bach, Mendelssohn, Schumann and Beethoven. Take the panoramic lift up to the unconquered hilltop fortress, Festung Königstein, for a breathtaking view of the Saxon Switzerland National Park. Come in December so you can stroll through Dresden's *striezelmarkt*, Germany's oldest Christmas market filled with traditional tastes and delights.

As Germany's bakery, where sweets and treats with coffee abound, this region produces noteworthy dinners. The cuisine is time-honored German cooking mingled with Sorbian and Bohemian cultures, which results in a delightful culinary experience, one that is easy to recreate at home.

Tafelspitz mit Meerrettich-Sosse

(BOILED BEEF WITH HORSERADISH SAUCE)

For fork-tender beef and an amazing beef broth, make this German classic that originated in Austria. The method is so simple and always works to get the beef super tender. It's important to remember that the meat needs to be completely plunged into boiling water to seal its pores. If the water is not boiling or the pot too small to submerge the meat, it will end up as tough as shoe leather. Choose your pot wisely as explained in the recipe and make sure your water is boiling, and you'll be rewarded with a mouthwatering roast every time. When it's served with the fresh horseradish sauce, this beef is a winner!

BEEF

1¼ lb (570 g) beef chuck or bottom round roast

6 cups (1.5 L) water, or as needed

1 tbsp (15 g) butter

1 large onion, unpeeled

2 large carrots, coarsely chopped

1 large leek, coarsely chopped

1 cup (227 g) cubed celeriac or 1 cup (100 g) coarsely chopped celery

1 tsp salt, plus more as needed

1 dried bay leaf

4 black peppercorns

2 cloves

HORSERADISH SAUCE

3 tbsp (45 g) butter

3 tbsp (24 g) all-purpose flour

½ cup (125 ml) broth from cooking the beef

½ cup (125 ml) milk

3 tbsp (45 g) freshly grated horseradish

Salt and freshly ground black pepper, as needed

To make the beef, choose a saucepan that is big enough to allow the roast to be fully submerged in water. Check the size by putting the roast in the saucepan and covering it with approximately 6 cups (1.5 L) of cold water, submerging the roast by at least 1 inch (2.5 cm). Then, remove the meat and measure how much water was used. Dry the saucepan. Prepare the roast by removing any excess fat and silver skin with a sharp knife.

Melt the butter in the saucepan over medium-high heat. Cut the onion in half and put the halves, flat-side down, in the saucepan and sauté for 2 to 3 minutes, or until the onion has lightly browned. Add the amount of water that was measured earlier when you submerged the roast and increase the heat to high. Bring the water to a boil. Add the roast and return to a boil. Add the carrots, leek, celeriac, salt, bay leaf, peppercorns and cloves. Let the water come to a boil again, reduce the heat to medium-low and skim off the foam that comes to the top. Cover the saucepan and simmer gently for 2 hours, or until the meat is tender. Ladle about 1 cup (250 ml) of broth through a sieve to use for making the sauce.

To make the horseradish sauce, melt the butter in a small skillet over medium heat. Whisk in the flour until no lumps remain and the roux is smooth, which will take about 1 minute, but do not let it brown. Whisk in the broth and milk until the sauce is creamy. Reduce the heat to medium-low and simmer for about 5 minutes. You may need to add more broth if the sauce becomes too thick. Stir in the horseradish, adding more if you like it hotter, and season with salt and pepper.

To serve, remove the meat from the broth, slice it and place the sauce on the side. Boiled potatoes are the traditional accompaniment for this.

Note: The extra broth can be used for making soup, especially Gaisburger Marsch (Beef and Veggie Stew; page 64).

Leipziger Allerlei

(VEGGIE STEW)

The most famous of Leipzig's dishes is this mixture of vegetables. The story behind it is varied, making the original ingredients a bit of a mystery as well. For some, it's a medley of just vegetables, cooked in a special way. For others, it also includes various seafood, including crawfish. For me, it's just veggies, and I cook it the easy way. Just as delicious and just as traditional. Traditional means "the way you've always done it" and *allerlei* means "a variety of," so this is a variety of veggies, just the way you like it.

If possible, use the freshest vegetables you can find. With the asparagus and sugar snap peas, that means this really is a spring dish. Add your own favorite veggies if you like, such as kohlrabi and green beans. Omit the ones you don't like and create your very own traditional *Leipziger Allerlei!*

2 cups (500 ml) beef broth

4 tbsp (60 g) butter, divided

1 tsp salt, plus more as needed

Pinch of sugar

2 cups (250 g) thinly sliced carrots

2 cups (300 g) fresh cauliflower florets

½ lb (227 g) green asparagus, cut into bite-sized pieces

1½ cups (120 g) sugar snap peas

2 cups (170 g) button or cremini mushrooms, thickly sliced

2 tbsp (16 g) all-purpose flour

½ cup (125 ml) heavy cream

Freshly ground white pepper, as needed

Freshly grated nutmeg, as needed

2 tbsp (5 g) finely chopped fresh parsley, for garnish

Combine the broth, 1 tablespoon (15 g) of the butter, salt and sugar in a large saucepan over high heat. Bring the broth to a boil and add the carrots. Cover the saucepan, reduce the heat to medium-high and simmer for 5 minutes. Add the cauliflower. Cover the saucepan and simmer for 5 minutes. Stir in the asparagus and the peas. Cover the saucepan and simmer for 5 minutes. Drain the vegetables, reserving the cooking liquid in a medium bowl. Put the vegetables in another medium bowl and cover the bowl to keep the vegetables warm. Measure the cooking liquid and add enough water to make 1½ cups (375 ml) to use for the sauce.

Melt 1 tablespoon (15 g) of the butter in the saucepan over medium heat and add the mushrooms. Cook for about 5 minutes to soften them. Transfer the mushrooms to the vegetables in the bowl. Melt the remaining 2 tablespoons (30 g) of the butter in the saucepan over medium heat and whisk in the flour. Continue stirring until the roux is smooth, which will take about 1 minute, but do not let it brown. Whisk in the reserved cooking liquid and simmer for about 5 minutes. Stir in the cream. Season the sauce with additional salt, pepper and nutmeg.

Gently stir the vegetables into the sauce and heat, but do not let the mixture simmer. Serve garnished with the parsley.

Oma's Ecke

The traditional method calls for cooking each vegetable separately in water with salt and butter. The veggies are then shocked in ice water and set aside. Once all are cooked, they are combined with the sauce and perhaps some crawfish and crawfish butter.

I prefer to cook the veggies together, adding them at different times so that they are tender at the same time. It's a bit easier to do it this way and makes the whole process just a bit faster.

Serves
4

Salzbraten

(PORK ROAST ON A BED OF SALT)

The Saxons like their Sunday roasts and this one, made throughout Germany, is easy to make. Using a pork shoulder for this, you'll be rewarded with tender and juicy slices, ready to be served not just on Sundays but throughout the week. It almost seems impossible that something so utterly simple could be so wonderfully delicious.

In fact, the first time you make this recipe, you'll wonder if that's all there is to it. You may also wonder if the meat is going to be too salty. Yes, this is all there is to it and no, it won't be too salty. Give this a try and you'll be making it again and again.

2 lbs (908 g) coarse kosher salt

2 lb (908 g) boneless pork shoulder or butt roast

2 tsp (10 ml) neutral oil

1 tsp salt

1 tsp freshly ground black pepper

3 tbsp (45 g) German whole-grain mustard

Preheat the oven to 350°F (175°C).

Line a rimmed baking sheet with foil. Spread the kosher salt on the foil to create a bed for the roast to lie on. It should be at least ½ inch (13 mm) thick and only needs to spread out a bit longer and wider than the roast itself.

Remove any excess fat from the outside of the roast. Rub the oil over the roast and then sprinkle it with the salt and pepper. Place the roast on the salt bed and spread the mustard over the top and sides of the roast.

Push the coarse salt up against the sides of the meat slightly. Place the baking sheet in the oven and roast for about 2 hours, or until the meat reaches 165°F (74°C). Do not open the oven during the roasting time. If the outside of the roast has not become crisp enough once it is roasted, increase the oven to 400°F (200°C) and leave the roast in the oven an extra 10 minutes to brown.

Transfer the roast to a platter and let it rest for 10 minutes before slicing. Do not cover the roast or the crust will become soggy. Cut the roast into thick slices and serve.

Oma's Ecke

Bavarians like to claim this recipe as their own. Perhaps, it is. And . . . perhaps not. The origins of this method are hard to establish. In other parts of the world, a slightly similar dish exists in which an actual salt crust is made that encases the roast, but in this recipe, the meat just sits on the salt.

Whether it comes from Saxony or Bavaria, this tastes wonderful with creamy Gestovte Kartoffeln (Creamed Potatoes; page 129) from Schleswig-Holstein, and of course, some extra German mustard.

Teichlmauke

(MASHED POTATO RING WITH BROTH, BEEF AND SAUERKRAUT)

In the dialect of Saxony, *teichl* means "pond" and *mauke* means "mash." With a mound of mashed potatoes holding a pond of broth with tender *tafelspitz* beef chunks in the middle, trying to be the last one who keeps the broth "pond" intact is always fun.

TAFELSPITZ BEEF

1 lb (454 g) beef chuck or bottom round roast

6 cups (1.5 L) water

1 large onion, coarsely chopped

1 large carrot, coarsely chopped

1 large leek, coarsely chopped

1 cup (227 g) cubed celeriac or 1 cup (100 g) coarsely chopped celery

1 tsp salt, plus more as needed

1 dried bay leaf

SAUERKRAUT

1 (28-oz [784-g]) can sauerkraut, rinsed and well drained

1½ cups (375 ml) beef broth

1 cup (150 g) diced onions

1 tsp caraway seeds

1 dried bay leaf

1 medium Yukon gold potato, peeled

Salt and freshly ground black pepper, as needed

MASHED POTATOES

1¾ lbs (800 g) peeled russet or Yukon gold potatoes, cubed

1 tsp salt, plus more as needed

1 tbsp (15 g) butter

4 oz (112 g) lean bacon, diced

1 cup (150 g) finely diced onions

1 cup (250 ml) broth from the beef

2 tbsp (5 g) finely chopped fresh parsley, for garnish

To make the beef, choose a saucepan that is big enough to allow the roast to be fully submerged. Check the size by putting the roast in the saucepan and covering it with approximately 6 cups (1.5 L) of cold water. Remove the roast and set it aside. Add the onion, carrot, leek, celeriac, salt and bay leaf to the same saucepan. Bring the mixture to a boil over high heat. Add the roast. Reduce the heat to low, bring the mixture to a simmer, cover the saucepan and simmer gently for 2 hours, or until the meat is tender.

To make the sauerkraut, put the sauerkraut, broth, onions, caraway seeds and bay leaf in a medium saucepan while the roast is cooking. Bring the mixture to a boil over high heat. Reduce the heat to low, cover the saucepan and simmer for 45 minutes. Remove the bay leaf and grate the potato into the sauerkraut. Cook for 10 minutes, stirring occasionally. Season with the salt and pepper. Cover the saucepan and keep the sauerkraut warm until ready to serve.

About 30 minutes before the meat is ready, prepare the mashed potatoes. Put the potatoes in another large saucepan, cover them with water, add the salt and bring the potatoes to a boil over high heat. Cover the saucepan, reduce the heat to medium-low and simmer until the potatoes are tender, about 15 minutes. Drain the potatoes.

Meanwhile, melt the butter in a small skillet over medium heat. Add the bacon and onions. Sauté for about 5 minutes, stirring occasionally, until the bacon fat has rendered and the onions are lightly caramelized.

Remove the roast from the broth and cut it into bite-sized pieces. Cover them to keep them warm. Strain the cooking broth into a large bowl, season it with salt and pepper and cover it to keep it warm. Mash the potatoes, adding about 1 cup (250 ml) of the broth, until the potatoes are smooth and creamy. Stir in the bacon and onion mixture. Season with salt, if needed.

To serve, put a mound of mashed potatoes on each plate. Using the ladle to make the pond, press an indentation in the middle of the potatoes, add the meat to the middle, fill the pond with the broth and garnish with the parsley. Serve with the sauerkraut on the side. The extra broth can be refrigerated or frozen to use in soups or stews.

Sachsen Anhalt

(Saxony-Anhalt)

Wander along the hiking trails in the Harz Mountains among the rugged granite cliffs and the misty moors, stopping off at ancient medieval towns, such as Quedlinburg (a UNESCO World Heritage site) with its thirteen hundred half-timbered houses. Hop on board the *Harzer Schmalspurbahn* (Harz Narrow Gauge Railway) and take a trip up the Brocken, the highest peak in northern Germany.

Follow the Sky Paths route that combines archaeological findings, including Germany's Stonehenge, the *Pömmelte Woodhenge*, with thousand-year-old astronomy and the *Nebra's Himmelsscheibe* (Sky Disc), the oldest concrete depiction of the heavens anywhere in the world.

As you travel through this region, filled with the most UNESCO World Cultural Heritage sites in Germany, and stop off to dine, you'll soon discover that root vegetables and cabbage dishes abound. Included in these is the world-renowned sauerkraut. But there is much more to Saxony-Anhalt's cuisine—and you will be pleasantly surprised.

Braunkohl und Klump

(KALE AND POTATO CASSEROLE)

Braunkohl is a type of ancient kale that is brownish-violet in color. It's a tall variety with its bottom leaves used as cattle feed and the top ones finding their way into the kitchen. When the green kale became popular, the old name remained, and today, *grünkohl* (literally "green cabbage," or kale) is still called *braunkohl* in this region. The *klump* part of this meal is actually a clump of potatoes; in other words, a dumpling.

The traditional recipe for this casserole included a kale-pear mixture, which is cooked for hours with fresh or smoked pork hocks. It was then covered with a grated raw potato clump (the dumpling) and baked on low for hours. Here, I've made it a bit different, more like a shepherd's pie, using mashed potatoes to cover a kale, pear and smoked sausage medley. A wonderful hearty meal that's perfect for a cold winter's day.

1¾ lbs (800 g) peeled russet or Yukon gold potatoes, quartered

1 tsp salt, plus more as needed

1 cup (250 ml) hot milk, or as needed

Freshly ground black pepper, as needed

Freshly grated nutmeg, as needed

2 tbsp (30 g) clarified butter or 2 tbsp (30 ml) neutral oil

2 cups (300 g) diced onions

1½ lbs (680 g) frozen kale (see *Oma's Ecke*)

1 lb (454 g) Bosc pears, peeled and thickly sliced

1½ lbs (680 g) smoked sausages, cut into ¼-inch (6-mm) slices

1 cup (250 ml) beef broth

1 cup (250 ml) water, if needed

1 tbsp (9 g) cornstarch mixed with 1 tbsp (15 ml) cold water, if needed

3 tbsp (45 g) butter, divided

Put the potatoes in a medium saucepan, cover them with water, add the salt and bring the water to a boil over high heat. Cover the saucepan, reduce the heat to medium-low and simmer for 20 minutes, or until the potatoes are tender. Drain and mash the potatoes using enough milk to get a smooth consistency. Season with additional salt, pepper and nutmeg.

While the potatoes are cooking, melt the butter in a large saucepan over medium heat. Add the onions and sauté until they are translucent, 5 to 7 minutes. Add the kale, pears, sausages and broth. Increase the heat to high and bring the mixture to a boil. Reduce the heat to medium-low, bring the mixture to a simmer and cover the saucepan. Cook for 15 minutes, stirring occasionally and adding the water, if needed. After 15 minutes, if the kale is too moist, stir just enough of the cornstarch slurry into the kale to thicken, which will take about 2 minutes. Season the mixture with salt and pepper.

While the potatoes and kale are cooking, preheat the oven to 400°F (200°C). Grease a 9 x 13-inch (23 x 33-cm) baking dish with 1 tablespoon (15 g) of the butter.

Spread the kale mixture into the baking dish. Cover the kale with a layer of the mashed potatoes and smooth the top. Cut the remaining 2 tablespoons (30 g) of the butter into small pieces and put them on the potatoes.

Bake the casserole for 20 to 30 minutes, or until the top is golden brown. Serve hot.

Oma's Ecke

I like to use frozen kale, but if you have fresh kale available, blanching it first helps with the final flavor. Trim the tough stalks from the leaves and cook the leaves in boiling water for 2 minutes. Shock them in ice water and drain. Coarsely chop the kale and use as directed in the recipe.

Sauerkrautsuppe

(SAUERKRAUT SOUP)

This is one of those easy *eintopf* (one-pot) meals that Germany is so famous for. Since everything is cooked in one pot, the cleanup is quick and easy. And since it's a soup, you do not need to be too accurate with your measurements. You can easily add some extra potatoes and broth if unexpected guests arrive. If perchance you have leftovers, the soup tastes even better the next day. Which means you can make this the day before you need it and rest assured you have awesomeness to serve.

When you do serve this soup, include some freshly baked, hot-out-of-the-oven, crusty bread to sop up all the deliciousness. This is a warming and hearty meal that highlights one of Germany's renowned ingredients: sauerkraut.

MEATBALLS

1 lb (454 g) lean ground beef
(see *Oma's Ecke*)

1 large egg

1 tsp mustard

½ tsp salt

¼ tsp black pepper

SOUP

3 tbsp (45 g) clarified butter or
3 tbsp (45 ml) neutral oil

1 cup (150 g) diced onions

2 tbsp (24 g) sugar

1 (28-oz [784-g]) can sauerkraut,
drained

1 tbsp (5 g) paprika

4 cups (1 L) beef broth

1 lb (454 g) peeled Yukon gold
potatoes, cut into 1-inch (2.5-cm)
cubes

8 oz (227 g) carrots, cut into
1-inch (2.5-cm) cubes

Salt and freshly ground black
pepper, as needed

4 tbsp (60 g) sour cream,
for garnish, optional

Make the meatballs by mixing the beef, egg, mustard, salt and pepper together in a medium bowl. Form the mixture into small meatballs and set them aside.

To make the soup, melt the butter in a large saucepan over medium heat. Add the onions and sauté for 5 to 7 minutes, or until the onions are tender. Add the sugar and sauté for 3 to 4 minutes, until the onions are golden brown. Add the sauerkraut and sauté for 3 to 5 minutes, until some of the sauerkraut has browned. Add the paprika and stir.

Add the beef broth and stir up any browned bits at the bottom of the saucepan. Add the meatballs, potatoes and carrots. Increase the heat to medium-high and bring the soup to a boil. Reduce the heat to medium-low, cover the saucepan and simmer for 20 to 30 minutes.

Season the soup with salt and pepper, if needed. Serve it in soup bowls, garnished with the sour cream, if desired.

Oma's Ecke

If you want to make this quickly, you can use 1 pound (454 g) of frozen cooked meatballs instead of making your own. There's no need to thaw them first. Simply replace your homemade ones with these.

Alternatively, you can use 1 pound (454 g) of your favorite raw beef or pork sausages. Simply cut the sausage links apart. Squeeze the meat out of each link, pinching to get the meatball shapes. Roll them slightly, if desired, and use these in place of the homemade meatballs.

Sauerkraut und Bratwurst

(SAUERKRAUT AND SAUSAGES)

It's hard to believe that fermented cabbage can be so delicious. With a totally non-German background, sauerkraut is now known worldwide with its German name. Perhaps it's because we love it so much that it finds its way into soups, stews, dumplings, breads and cakes. Here, though, it's a side dish that's a perfect accompaniment to *bratwurst*, one of more than a thousand different sausages types available in Germany. If you can't find *bratwurst* where you live, substitute your favorite raw sausage.

SAUERKRAUT

2 tbsp (30 g) clarified butter or
2 tbsp (30 ml) neutral oil or bacon drippings

1 cup (150 g) minced onions

4 oz (112 g) lean slab bacon, cut into ¼-inch (6-mm) pieces

1 (28-oz [784-g]) can sauerkraut, rinsed and well drained

1½ cups (375 ml) beef broth, apple juice or white wine, divided

1 tsp caraway seeds

1 dried bay leaf

Pinch of sugar

Salt and freshly ground black pepper, as needed

SAUSAGES

4 raw bratwurst sausages

1 to 2 tbsp (15 to 30 ml) clarified butter or neutral oil

To make the sauerkraut, melt the butter in a large saucepan over medium heat. Add the onions and bacon and cook, stirring occasionally, until the bacon fat has rendered and the onions are translucent, 5 to 7 minutes. Add the sauerkraut and fry for 3 to 5 minutes, until some of the sauerkraut has browned.

Add 1 cup (250 ml) of the broth, the caraway seeds and the bay leaf. Stir, increase the heat to high and bring the broth to a boil. Reduce the heat to medium-low, cover the saucepan and simmer for at least 20 minutes and up to 60 minutes, depending on how tender you like the sauerkraut. Stir occasionally, adding the remaining ½ cup (125 ml) of the broth, if necessary.

While the sauerkraut is cooking, prepare the bratwurst. Put the bratwurst in a medium saucepan and cover them with water. Bring the water to a boil over medium-high heat. Reduce the heat to low and simmer for 10 minutes. Drain and place the bratwurst on paper towels to dry.

Melt the butter in a medium skillet over medium-high heat. Add the bratwurst and fry on each side, until they are nicely browned on all sides, about 5 minutes. The internal temperature should be 160°F (71°C).

Finish the sauerkraut by removing the bay leaf and seasoning it with the sugar and salt and pepper (see *Oma's Ecke*). Serve the sauerkraut and sausages with German mustard on the side and some rye bread or mashed potatoes.

Oma's Ecke

If you find the cooked sauerkraut is too moist, stir in some cornstarch (about 1 tablespoon [9 g]) dissolved in a bit of cold water. Add just enough of this slurry to get the sauerkraut as thick as you like. Let it simmer for 1 minute before serving. Alternatively, just leave the lid off and turn up the heat to evaporate the excess liquid. You will need to keep stirring so it doesn't burn on the bottom of the pot.

Schusterpfanne

("SHOEMAKER'S PAN")

The origins of this recipe are quite vague, but the name seems to stem from the unusual appearance of the dish when it is made in a casserole and layered in a certain manner. Viewed from above, it resembles a shoe. Traditionally, the meat was boiled as a single piece and put into the middle of the dish. I do mine just a bit differently. I like to cube and brown the meat first, making for a richer and meatier flavor. It's also easier to serve right from the dish this way.

2 lb (908 g) boneless pork shoulder or butt, cut into 1-inch (2.5-cm) cubes

Salt and freshly ground black pepper, as needed

2 tbsp (30 g) clarified butter or 2 tbsp (30 ml) neutral oil

3 cups (750 ml) beef or chicken broth

2 lbs (908 g) peeled firm pears (such as Bosc), cut into ½-inch (13-mm) slices

2 lbs (908 g) peeled Yukon gold potatoes, cut into ½-inch (13-mm) slices

1 tsp caraway seeds

Pinch of ground cloves and sugar

2 to 3 sprigs fresh thyme

Preheat the oven to 400°F (200°C). Grease a 9 x 13-inch (23 x 33-cm) baking dish.

Sprinkle the pork lightly with salt and pepper. Melt the butter in a large saucepan over medium-high heat. Brown the pork on all sides, 8 to 10 minutes, working in batches so as not to crowd the meat. Remove the pork from the saucepan and pile it in the center of the baking dish. Pour the broth into the saucepan and scrape up any browned bits. Remove the saucepan from the heat and set it aside.

Layer the pears on one end of the baking dish, surrounding the meat on one side. Layer the potatoes on the other end of the dish, surrounding the meat on that side. As you look down at the dish, the meat would be the center inside of the shoe, the pears would be the heel and the potatoes the toes.

Pour the hot broth over the top of the mixture so that it comes no more than halfway up the potatoes and pears. Sprinkle the potatoes lightly with salt. Sprinkle the caraways seeds over the potatoes and the pork. Sprinkle the cloves and sugar over the pears. Lay the thyme over the potatoes.

Cover the baking dish with its lid or foil and put it in the oven. Bake for 40 minutes. Uncover and bake for 15 to 20 minutes, or until the potatoes are slightly browned and tender.

Serve the Schusterpfanne directly from the baking dish in large soup bowls, perhaps with a green side salad.

Oma's Ecke

If you wish, you can make this dish more like a stew. Layer everything together in the baking dish and bake it as directed in the recipe. However, trying to recognize it as a shoe is part of the fun. Do not tell your guests what it's supposed to look like but let them guess. All will be winners when it comes to enjoying this unusual meal.

Tiegelbraten

(BEEF AND LAMB POT)

Literal translations sometimes do not work, because *tiegelbraten* would then be a pot roast—and that is totally what this is not. *Tiegel* is a special type of pot that this mixed meat dish was served in, especially for wedding breakfasts. *Braten* is a roast that has been roasted, yet a *tiegelbraten* is not roasted but rather braised.

The original dish, using whole roasts, strains the onions out and does not include them in the final dish. However, by searing the meat cubes and the onions together, a lovely complexity of flavors develops. This is usually served without thickening the gravy. Personally, I like to thicken it, making it just a touch richer. Another popular addition that is delicious is to sprinkle cheese over the top and let that get bubbly and brown in the oven. Served with crusty white bread, the wedding breakfast is complete. Served with potatoes, dinner is ready.

3 tbsp (45 g) clarified butter or 3 tbsp (45 ml) neutral oil

¾ lb (340 g) boneless lamb, cut into ¾-inch (2-cm) cubes (see *Oma's Ecke*)

2 lb (908 g) boneless beef sirloin steak, cut into ¾-inch (2-cm) cubes

2 cups (300 g) diced onions

4 cups (1 L) hot beef broth

2 dried bay leaves

½ tsp salt, plus more as needed

4 tbsp (60 g) butter

4 tbsp (32 g) all-purpose flour

Freshly ground black pepper, as needed

¾ lb (340 g) Emmental or Gouda cheese, grated

Oma's Ecke

Traditionally, this is made with a half-and-half mixture of beef and lamb. I prefer making it with just beef, a delicious twist on the original. You could even substitute some boneless pork chops for the lamb.

This recipe can be prepared in an oven-safe 11-inch (28-cm) skillet to prepare the entire dish, or a 9 x 13-inch (23 x 33-cm) baking dish can be used for the final baking stage.

Melt the clarified butter in the skillet over medium-high heat. Add the lamb and beef and brown the meat on all sides, 8 to 10 minutes, working in batches and being careful not to crowd the meat. Transfer the browned meat to a large bowl. Add the onions to the skillet, reduce the heat to medium and sauté for 5 to 7 minutes, or until the onions are translucent. Add the broth, stirring up any browned bits from the bottom. Return the meat and any accumulated juices to the skillet. Add the bay leaves and salt. Increase the heat to medium-high and bring the mixture to a boil. Reduce the heat to medium-low, cover the skillet and simmer for 45 minutes, or until the meat is tender.

Preheat the oven to 450°F (232°C).

Using a slotted spoon, transfer the meat and most of the onions to another large bowl and strain the cooking liquid to use for the gravy. Remove the bay leaves.

Melt the butter in the skillet over medium heat and whisk in the flour. Continue stirring until the roux is smooth, which will take about 1 minute, but do not let it brown. Whisk in about 3 cups (750 ml) of the strained cooking liquid and simmer until the gravy is thickened, about 2 minutes, adding a bit more liquid if the gravy is too thick. Stir in the meat with the onions and season with salt and pepper.

Keep the meat, onions and gravy in the skillet if it is oven-safe. If not, transfer it to the baking dish. Sprinkle the cheese evenly over the top. Bake for 15 minutes, until the top is bubbly and the cheese has browned.

The *Tiegelbraten* is ready to serve with crusty white bread for dunking or with potatoes that have been garnished with chopped parsley.

Mecklenburg Vorpommern

Mecklenburg-Vorpommern is home to more than two thousand lakes, making it one of Germany's leading destinations for holiday seekers and tourists alike. Add 1,200 miles (2,000 km) of coastline, and you just know that anything water related will be amazing. Sailing. Canoeing. Rafting. Kiting. Beach parties.

This state is also home to more than two thousand palaces, castles and manor houses, many hidden among the solitary lakes. Roam through the historic town centers of Wismar and Stralsund with their Gothic brickwork buildings (which are UNESCO World Heritage sites) and stroll through the capital, Schwerin, with its fairy-tale castle. Wander through the museums, such as the one in Stralsund displaying Viking gold or the one in Tribsees, the *Vorpommersches Kartoffelmuseum*, a museum dedicated to the celebrated potato.

The traditional cuisine of this northeast corner of Germany is affected by what is caught in the lakes, what is hunted in the forests and what is grown in the fertile soil. They are hearty, down-to-earth dishes, many of them made with root crops (such as the lowly rutabagas and potatoes). Fish is common. Beets are popular. Pork is king.

Blumenkohl-Bombe

(CAULIFLOWER BOMB WITH MINCE AND BACON)

The first time anyone sees the large, flat-bottomed, bacon-covered "ball" sitting in the middle of the dining room table, imaginations run wild. Once it is cut into pieces just like a cake and served, the inside is such a surprise. Once it is tasted, a normal meatloaf and cauliflower side dish become a thing of the past.

Simply speaking, this is a whole cauliflower, covered with a meatloaf mixture, wrapped with bacon and roasted to perfection. It is a hearty, down-to-earth meal that needs only some boiled potatoes on the side and the sauce to dunk everything in. Leftovers, if there are any, heat up wonderfully the next day.

1 (2-lb [908-g]) head cauliflower (see *Oma's Ecke*)

2½ tsp (13 g) salt, divided, plus more as needed

2 lbs (908 g) lean ground beef (see *Oma's Ecke*)

1 cup (150 g) diced onions

3 large eggs

½ tsp freshly ground black pepper, plus more as needed

½ tsp paprika

½ cup (60 g) breadcrumbs

12 oz (335 g) sliced lean bacon

4 tbsp (60 g) butter

4 tbsp (32 g) all-purpose flour

1 to 2 tbsp (15 to 30 g) German or yellow mustard

Freshly grated nutmeg, as needed

Oma's Ecke

When precooking the cauliflower, use a pot that is not made of iron or aluminum, or else your cauliflower may turn yellowish. Stainless steel works best. For the meatloaf, you can use a mixture of beef and pork, if you wish.

Preheat the oven to 360°F (180°C) and grease a large baking dish or rimmed baking sheet.

Prepare the cauliflower by removing the leaves and cutting the stalk close to the florets, being careful not to cut into them. The cauliflower should be able to sit flat on the work surface. Carefully cut an **X** into the stalk end to help speed up the cooking time. The cauliflower needs to remain whole.

Put the cauliflower in a large pot and add hot water until it is covered. Add 1 teaspoon of the salt and bring the water to a boil over high heat. Reduce the heat to medium and simmer for 10 minutes. Lift out the cauliflower and put it in the prepared baking dish stalk-side down. Measure 3 cups (750 ml) of the cooking liquid and set it aside.

In a large bowl, combine the beef, onions, eggs, remaining 1½ teaspoons (8 g) of salt, pepper, paprika and breadcrumbs. Mix gently with your hands. Taking a handful of the mixture, press it gently against the cauliflower to make a layer about 1 inch (2.5 cm) thick. Continue this process until the entire cauliflower is covered and all the meat is used. Cover the entire bomb with the bacon slices. Press the bacon onto the meat, overlapping them if needed to entirely cover the meat mixture. Place the bomb in the oven, uncovered, and roast for 70 to 80 minutes, or until the bacon is nicely crisped.

Meanwhile, make the sauce by melting the butter in a medium skillet over medium heat. Whisk in the flour until the roux is smooth, which will take about 1 minute, but do not let it brown. Gradually whisk in 2 cups (500 ml) of the reserved cooking liquid and continue cooking and stirring until the sauce is smooth. Cook for 5 minutes, adding more of the reserved cooking liquid if the sauce gets too thick. Add the mustard, and season with salt, pepper and nutmeg. Cover the skillet and keep the sauce warm until ready to serve.

Place the cauliflower bomb on a serving dish. Slice it into sections (just like a cake) and serve it with the sauce.

Hühnerfrikassee

(CHICKEN FRICASSEE)

Making this will have you thinking you are right back in *oma*'s kitchen. She would take leftover chicken and mix it with whatever was found in the fridge to create a delicious fricassee. This "leftover dish" now graces the menus in even the best German restaurants.

Just like me, you'll be cooking extra chicken in order to have leftovers to make this (or you can even use a purchased rotisserie chicken). If you want to start from scratch, put about 1 pound (454 g) of raw chicken breasts in a medium saucepan and cover them with boiling chicken broth or water. Add ½ teaspoon of salt and simmer gently over low heat, covered, for at least 15 minutes, skimming off any foam that forms on the top. The internal temperature should be 165°F (74°C). Use the meat and its broth for the fricassee.

4 tbsp (60 g) butter, divided

8 oz (227 g) button or cremini mushrooms, thickly sliced

4 tbsp (32 g) all-purpose flour

4 cups (1 L) hot chicken broth

1 cup (150 g) frozen green peas, thawed

1 (15-oz [420-g]) can white asparagus, drained, cut into 1½-inch (4-cm) slices

4 cups (500 g) cooked cubed chicken meat

Salt and freshly ground black pepper, as needed

1 large egg yolk mixed with 4 tbsp (60 ml) heavy cream

2 tbsp (5 g) finely chopped fresh parsley or chives, for garnish

In a large saucepan over medium-high heat, melt 2 tablespoons (30 g) of the butter and add the mushrooms. Sauté them for 4 to 5 minutes, until they are lightly browned. Remove the mushrooms and set them aside.

Make a roux by melting the remaining 2 tablespoons (30 g) of the butter in the saucepan, lowering the heat to medium and whisking in the flour. Continue stirring until the roux is smooth, which will take about 1 minute, but do not let it brown. Whisk in the broth and stir until smooth. Return the mushrooms to the sauce, cover the saucepan and simmer for about 5 minutes.

Add the peas, asparagus and chicken. Simmer for 3 to 4 minutes, until the peas are cooked. Season with the salt and pepper. Take the saucepan off the heat and immediately stir in the egg yolk mixture.

Serve the Hühnerfrikassee garnished with the parsley and a side of rice.

One of the fun things I love to do in the kitchen is to make small changes to traditional recipes. Sometimes it doesn't work out. Often it does.

For this recipe, here are a few interesting additions to try: Add 1 teaspoon of capers to the finished sauce. Or add a bit of zip by including 1 tablespoon (15 ml) of fresh lemon juice. Add extra spices if you wish—paprika, cayenne pepper or nutmeg. Use a mix of green peas and carrots or frozen cauliflower florets instead of just peas. Omit the asparagus, or use green asparagus instead. Each of these will make your traditional dish something totally different.

Rote-Bete-Suppe mit Stampfkartoffeln

(RED BEET SOUP WITH MASHED POTATOES)

This recipe entered my life the day I married my hubby. It's still a favorite of his and it was always fun to make when our boys were young. I'd serve each member of the family the bright red soup in a bowl alongside a plate with bacony mashed potatoes and eggs sunny-side up. One would take a spoon, half-filled with potatoes, and dip it into the soup bowl to enjoy both in one mouthful. Fun memories!

2 lbs (908 g) peeled russet potatoes, quartered

1 tsp salt, plus more as needed

2 tbsp (30 g) butter, divided

4 oz (112 g) bacon, diced

1 cup (150 g) diced onions

4 cups (680 g) canned sliced red beets, drained (see *Oma's Ecke*)

4 cups (1 L) beef broth

1 tsp sugar

1 tbsp (15 ml) pure white vinegar

Freshly ground black pepper, as needed

1 cup (250 ml) hot milk, or as needed

6 large eggs

4 tbsp (60 g) sour cream, for garnish

Put the potatoes in a large saucepan, cover them with water, add the salt and bring the potatoes to a boil over high heat. Reduce the heat to medium-low, cover the saucepan and simmer until the potatoes are tender, about 20 minutes. Drain the potatoes.

Meanwhile, in a small skillet over medium heat, melt 1 tablespoon (15 g) of the butter. Add the bacon and sauté for about 5 minutes, until the fat has rendered. Transfer the bacon to a small bowl. Add the remaining 1 tablespoon (15 g) of the butter to the skillet, then add the onions. Sauté the onions for 5 to 7 minutes, or until they are translucent.

Put the beets, sautéed onions and broth in a blender. Blend the ingredients until they are smooth, then pour the puree into a medium saucepan over medium heat. Alternatively, put them in a saucepan and use an immersion blender to create a puree. Simmer the puree for 5 minutes. Add the sugar and vinegar. Season with salt and pepper, adding more sugar and vinegar, if desired. Set the saucepan aside and keep it warm.

Mash the potatoes, using enough milk to achieve the consistency you like. Stir in the bacon. Season with salt and pepper. Fry the eggs in the skillet over medium heat for 2 to 3 minutes, so that they are sunny-side up.

Serve each person a bowl of soup garnished with a dollop of the sour cream and a plate with mashed potatoes and a fried egg on the side. Alternatively, make a mound of mashed potatoes on each plate. Using a ladle, make an indentation in the middle large enough to hold the soup. Fill the "pond" with soup and serve the eggs on the side.

Oma's Ecke

Fresh beets? Roast, sprinkled with olive oil and covered at 425°F (218°C) for 1 hour. Cool, peel and use.

Steckrübeneintopf

(RUTABAGA STEW)

Called *gestovte wruken* in the dialect of Mecklenburg-Vorpommern, this dish is a delicious way to use the lowly rutabaga, also known as a swede. Originally considered food for animals and *arme leute* (poor folk), it has recently gained a foothold, even in fancy restaurants. And why not? It has a peppery, earthy taste, being a cross between a cabbage and a turnip. Here, I have simmered it in a bacon-infused broth along with a mix of veggies to turn it into a delightful, hearty stew.

1 medium bunch fresh parsley

2 tbsp (30 g) clarified butter or 2 tbsp (30 ml) neutral oil

4 oz (112 g) lean slab bacon, cut into ¼-inch (6-mm) cubes

1 cup (150 g) diced onions

2 large carrots, cut into ½-inch (13-mm) cubes

1 large leek, cut into ½-inch (13-mm) slices

1 cup (227 g) cubed celeriac or 1 cup (100 g) coarsely chopped celery

4 cups (1 L) hot beef broth

2 lbs (908 g) rutabagas, cut into ½-inch (13-mm) cubes

1 lb (454 g) Yukon gold potatoes, peeled and cut into ½-inch (13-mm) cubes

1 tsp dried marjoram

1 dried bay leaf

Salt and freshly ground black pepper, as needed

½ lb (227 g) smoked sausage, cut into ¼-inch (6-mm) slices

Mince the parsley, reserving 1 tablespoon (5 g) for garnish.

Melt the butter in a large saucepan over medium heat. Add the bacon and onions and cook, stirring occasionally, until the bacon fat is rendered and the onions are translucent, 5 to 7 minutes. Add the carrots, leek, celeriac and parsley. Sauté for 5 minutes, stirring occasionally. Add the broth, stirring to loosen any browned bits at the bottom of the saucepan. Add the rutabagas, potatoes, marjoram and bay leaf.

Bring the mixture to a boil, reduce the heat to medium-low, cover the saucepan and simmer for 30 minutes, or until the vegetables are tender. Remove the bay leaf and season the stew with salt and pepper. Add the sausage and simmer for 2 to 3 minutes to heat through.

Serve the stew garnished with the reserved parsley.

Oma's Ecke

Bundled *suppengrün* (soup greens) can be conveniently purchased throughout Germany. The paper-wrapped bundle usually contains one or two carrots, one leek, a quarter of a celeriac and a bunch of parsley. Sometimes you will find that onions and other herbs are included, depending on which region you are in.

This *suppengrün* is Germany's version of *mirepoix* (flavor base consisting of diced carrots, onions and celery) and is frequently used when cooking soups and broths to enhance the flavor.

Thüring
(Thuringia)

Known as "the Green Heart of Germany," Thüringen has almost endless forests and more the 10,000 miles (16,000 km) of marked hiking trails, including a treetop trail through the canopy of the Hainich National Park (a UNESCO World Heritage site), one of the last primeval forests in Central Europe.

Castles and palaces abound as well. The most famous is Wartburg Castle (also a UNESCO World Heritage site), where Martin Luther stayed during his exile. Visit Weimar, which was designated the Cultural Capital of Europe for 1999, and tour the dozens of museums and galleries that celebrate greatness—think Goethe, Schiller, Liszt, Gropius and the list goes on.

Now, think food. Thüringer bratwurst's original 1613 recipe is kept in Weimar's State Archive, so a visit to the *Bratwurstmuseum* in Holzhausen would be delicious. Then, there is the potato dumpling. After all, "a Sunday without dumplings is no Sunday at all," according to the Thuringians. That works for me, as long as there is *rouladen* gravy (page 180)!

Rouladen

(BEEF ROLLS)

When it comes to this *oma*'s opinion, the most traditional German meal just has to be *rouladen* (elsewhere called roulade), potato dumplings and red cabbage. Tender beef with a gravy that far surpasses any other, this meal shouts celebration. Yes, it's a bit of work—but it's so worth it.

Finding the right cut of meat is usually a challenge. You can ask your butcher to cut ¼-inch (6-mm) thick slices of beef top round for you. If you do find precut slices and they are thicker, you can pound them to the right thickness once you have them at home.

4 (6- to 7-oz [170- to 200-g]) slices beef roulade

Salt and freshly ground black pepper, as needed

4 tsp (20 g) mustard

4 slices lean bacon, cut into halves

1 medium onion, thinly sliced

2 large garlic dill pickles, thinly sliced

2 tbsp (30 g) clarified butter or 2 tbsp (30 ml) neutral oil

1½ cups (375 ml) hot beef broth

2 tbsp (19 g) cornstarch mixed with 2 tbsp (30 ml) cold water

Set some metal skewers, kitchen twine or roulade clips near your workspace for easy access.

If the beef is thicker than ¼ inch (6 mm), pound it thinner. Place the meat slices on a clean work surface. Sprinkle the beef with salt and pepper. Turn the meat over and spread 1 teaspoon of mustard on each slice. Lay 2 half-slices of bacon over each slice. Distribute the onion and pickle slices at one end of each roulade. Starting at that end, roll up the roulade, turning in the sides to keep the filling inside. Use skewers to keep the roulade closed or bind them with kitchen twine.

Melt the butter over medium-high heat in a medium saucepan. Brown the rouladen well on all sides, 5 to 8 minutes. Pour in the broth and stir up any browned bits on the bottom of the saucepan. Reduce the heat to medium-low, cover the saucepan and simmer for about 1½ hours.

Place the roulade on a serving plate, remove the skewers and cover the plate to keep the roulade warm.

To make the gravy, bring the cooking liquid to a simmer. Stir in just enough of the cornstarch slurry to thicken the gravy, which will take about 2 minutes. Season the gravy with salt and pepper and serve alongside the Rouladen.

Oma's Ecke

There are many variations for filling the *rouladen,* and most people are quite adamant what should be in them and what should not. Some leave out the pickles. Some add sliced green bell peppers. Some insist on using Black Forest ham instead of bacon. Some sauté the onions first or dice the bacon and sauté it with the onions. Some add sour cream to the gravy. All of these variations are delicious.

If you want an easy alternative that tastes like *rouladen*, but without all the work, check out Flatladen ("Flat *Rouladen*"; page 183), my own method for making this an easy weeknight meal.

Flatladen

("FLAT ROULADEN")

Everyone in our family loves *Rouladen* (Beef Rolls; page 180). However, with the expense for the right kind of meat and the work involved in pounding and making the meat rolls, this meal has always been reserved for special occasions. That is, until I created Flatladen, the name our boys gave to my "flat *rouladen*." We now enjoy all the taste of the traditional *rouladen*, even on weeknights, without the fuss or expense. A win-win!

Depending on which part of Germany you're from, the fillings for *rouladen* differ. Mine always have bacon, onions, pickles and mustard in them, and my Flatladen have the same as well. You can alter my recipe to match what's in your *rouladen*.

1¾ lb (800 g) bottom round roast

3 tbsp (45 g) butter

6 slices bacon

1 cup (150 g) diced onions

3 cups (750 ml) hot water

4 large garlic dill pickles, thickly sliced

2 tbsp (30 g) German whole-grain mustard

½ tsp salt

½ tsp freshly ground black pepper

1 lb (454 g) button or cremini mushrooms, quartered, optional

3 tbsp (28 g) cornstarch mixed with 3 tbsp (45 ml) cold water

Prepare the roast by cutting it into approximately 2 x ¾-inch (5 x 2-cm) chunks.

Melt the butter in a large saucepan over medium-high heat. Add the bacon and fry for 5 minutes, or until the bacon fat has rendered and the bacon is crispy. Remove the bacon and reserve it for other purposes. Add about one-third of the beef to the hot fat in the saucepan (making sure not to crowd the saucepan) and brown it well on all sides, 5 to 8 minutes. Transfer the browned beef to a medium bowl. Continue browning the remaining beef in batches, being careful not to crowd the saucepan. Transfer each batch of cooked meat to the bowl.

Add the onions to the saucepan, reduce the heat to medium and sauté for 8 to 10 minutes, or until they are lightly browned. Add some of the hot water, stirring to loosen the browned bits from the bottom of the saucepan. Return the meat to the pan, along with any accumulated juices. Add the pickles, mustard, salt, pepper and just enough of the remaining hot water to almost cover the meat. Stir gently. Increase the heat to high and bring the mixture to a simmer. Reduce the heat to medium-low and cover the saucepan. Simmer for 1 hour. Add the mushrooms (if using). Simmer for 30 minutes, or until the meat is tender.

Stir in just enough of the cornstarch slurry to the simmering gravy to thicken it, which will take about 2 minutes.

Season the gravy with salt and pepper. If you have cut the meat into large pieces, take them out of the gravy, place them on a plate and serve the gravy on the side.

Since this makes a large quantity of delicious *rouladen* gravy, I freeze the leftovers to use later or to add to other recipes when needed. Even better is when I double the recipe. Then, to the leftovers, I will add leftover potatoes and vegetables, such as green beans, and turn the Flatladen into a stew for the next day. Making Hoppel Poppel (Potato and Egg Hash; page 14) the next day is a delicious alternative over which to pour the extra gravy.

Serves 4

Apfel-Rotkohl

(RED CABBAGE WITH APPLES)

One of the most traditional of all vegetable dishes throughout Germany is this sweet and sour red cabbage. Perfectly at home beside Rouladen (Beef Rolls; page 180), Sauerbraten (Marinated Braised Beef; page 22), roasts, poultry and game, it's as common at a fancy restaurant as it is in *oma*'s kitchen.

Since red cabbage can be used to dye yarn and Easter eggs, you'll need to protect your fingers and the cutting surface from the red juices. Using disposable gloves and an inexpensive plastic cutting board is the easiest way to do this.

3 tbsp (45 g) butter or 3 tbsp (45 ml) bacon fat

2 cups (300 g) finely diced onions

2 large Cortland or Granny Smith apples, peeled and diced

1¾ to 2 lb (800 to 908 g) red cabbage, shredded

1 tbsp (12 g) sugar

1 tsp salt, plus more as needed

¼ tsp freshly ground black pepper, plus more as needed

¼ tsp ground cloves (see *Oma's Ecke*)

3 juniper berries, optional

1 dried bay leaf

2 tbsp (30 ml) red wine vinegar

½ cup (125 ml) fresh orange juice, optional

1 cup (250 ml) water

2 tbsp (19 g) cornstarch mixed with 2 tbsp (30 ml) cold water

2 tbsp (30 ml) red currant jelly, optional

Melt the butter in a large saucepan over medium heat. Add the onions and sauté for 5 to 7 minutes, stirring occasionally, until they are lightly caramelized. Add the apples and sauté for 2 minutes.

Add the cabbage, sugar, salt, pepper, cloves, juniper berries (if using), bay leaf and vinegar. Add the orange juice (if using) and water. Stir the mixture and bring it to a simmer. Cover the saucepan, reduce the heat to low and simmer for 1 hour, stirring occasionally and adding a bit more water, if necessary.

Stir the cornstarch slurry into the cabbage a little bit at a time, until the cooking juices have thickened. Add the jelly (if using) and season with additional salt and pepper. Add extra vinegar and ground cloves if you prefer a spicier taste. Remove the bay leaf and serve.

Oma's Ecke

My *mutti* had a little trick up her sleeve. Since she only had whole cloves and no way to grind them, she'd take an onion and cut it in half through the middle. She'd poke the stems of the whole cloves into the cut part of the onion. The clove-studded onion halves would go into the red cabbage for the entire cooking time. At the end, the onions with the cloves would be removed.

As a young wife, I forgot to do this and added the whole cloves to the red cabbage. The taste was wonderful. However, biting into a cooked clove was not much fun. Since then, I've used ground cloves and sautéed the diced onion instead so that it remains in the cabbage. If you do plan on doing the clove-studded-onion trick, you will need to use 4 to 6 cloves to get the same flavor.

Thüringer Klösse

Serves 4

(POTATO DUMPLINGS FROM RAW POTATOES)

There are two different Thüringer dumplings called by the same name. The first uses one part cooked potatoes to two parts raw grated ones. The other, the one I grew up with, uses just raw potatoes, a very old recipe from my *mutti*. I recall spending what seemed like hours peeling and grating pounds of potatoes on Sundays. But all the work was worth it. Especially when served with her Rouladen (Beef Rolls; page 180) and gravy!

There's only one problem with this recipe. It takes practice to know what the dough should feel like. How much moisture to wring out of the potatoes and if extra potato flour is needed are learned techniques. Perfect them and you'll be rewarded with the delicious dumplings I grew up with.

2 slices white bread (see *Oma's Ecke*)

4 tbsp (60 g) butter, divided

3½ tsp (18 g) salt, divided

1 cup (250 ml) milk

4 tbsp (45 g) plain farina, such as Cream of Wheat brand

2¼ lb (1 kg) peeled Yukon gold potatoes

4 tbsp (43 g) potato flour, or as needed

Oma's Ecke

Why add the croutons? They assure that the dumplings do not have an uncooked center and add a wonderful buttery taste. If you have purchased croutons for a salad, they can be used here instead. Leftover dumplings are great cut into halves and reheated in any leftover gravy or sliced and fried in butter the next day.

Cut the bread into ½-inch (13-mm) cubes. Melt 1 tablespoon (15 g) of the butter in a medium skillet over medium heat. Add the bread cubes and fry them for about 5 minutes, tossing or stirring several times until all sides are toasted. Transfer these croutons to a plate and set aside.

Fill a large pot with about 3 quarts (2.8 L) of water and add 3 teaspoons (15 g) of the salt. Bring the water to a boil over high heat. Reduce the heat to low, cover the pot and keep the water at a very gentle simmer.

Put the milk, the remaining 3 tablespoons (45 g) of the butter and the remaining ½ teaspoon of salt in a small saucepan over high heat. Bring the mixture to a boil. Reduce the heat to low and add the farina, stirring for 3 to 5 minutes, until it has thickened. Remove the saucepan from the heat. Cover it to keep it warm.

Using the fine side of a box grater, grate the potatoes into a large bowl. Put the potatoes in the middle of a clean dish towel. Bring the ends of the towel together and twist the bottom with the potatoes. Squeeze out as much liquid as possible, catching the liquid in the bowl.

Dump the potatoes in another large, dry bowl and loosen the mass with a fork. Carefully pour off the strained water from the other bowl, keeping the settled potato starch in the bowl. Scrape the starch out from the bowl and add it to the potato mass. Stir in the hot farina and mix well. Once it is mixed, use your hands to finish mixing it, adding the potato flour if the mixture is too soft.

Form fist-size dumplings with your hands (moisten your hands to keep the potato dough from sticking), inserting 1 or 2 croutons in the center of each. Carefully lower the dumplings into the barely simmering salted water. Cook the dumplings, uncovered, for 20 minutes. The dumplings should float to the top, indicating that they are done. Remove them with a slotted spoon and serve.

Gulasch mit Pilze

(GOULASH WITH MUSHROOMS)

For generations, the forests in Thüringen provided wild meat and mushrooms that to this day are still enjoyed by many, especially in this dish. Here, though, instead of the deer, wild boar or rabbit, beef is used to provide a tender meat and the dark, rich gravy that's so loved, not only by the Thuringians, but throughout Germany and abroad.

3 tbsp (45 g) clarified butter or
3 tbsp (45 ml) neutral oil, divided

½ lb (227 g) lean slab bacon,
cut in ¼-inch (6-mm) cubes

1 lb (454 g) onions, thickly sliced

1¾ lb (800 g) beef round or chuck
roast, cut in ¾-inch (2-cm) cubes

2 tbsp (32 g) tomato paste

2 tbsp (16 g) all-purpose flour

2 cups (500 ml) beef broth

2 tsp (4 g) paprika

1 tsp salt, plus more as needed

½ lb (227 g) button mushrooms,
quartered

⅓ cup (80 ml) heavy cream

Freshly ground black pepper,
as needed

2 tbsp (5 g) finely chopped fresh
parsley, for garnish

Melt 2 tablespoons (30 g) of the butter in a large saucepan over medium heat. Add the bacon and the onions and sauté for 5 to 7 minutes, or until the onion is translucent. Transfer the bacon and onion to a large bowl and set aside.

Melt the remaining 1 tablespoon (15 g) of the butter in the same saucepan over medium-high heat. Add about one-third of the beef (making sure not to crowd the saucepan) and brown well on all sides, 5 to 8 minutes. Transfer the browned beef to a large bowl. Continue browning the rest in batches, being careful not to crowd the meat. Stir in the tomato paste and sauté for 1 minute. Return the bacon, onion and all the beef to the pan along with any accumulated juices, stirring to keep the ingredients from burning on the bottom.

Sprinkle the flour over everything and mix well. Pour in the broth, stirring up all the browned bits at the bottom of the saucepan. Add the paprika and salt. Bring to a simmer, cover the saucepan, reduce the heat to medium-low and simmer for 1 hour. Add the mushrooms and stir to make sure the goulash does not settle on the bottom of the saucepan and burn. If too much liquid has evaporated, add a bit of water. Cover and simmer for 30 minutes.

Stir in the cream, season with the pepper and additional salt if needed. Garnish with the parsley just before serving.

Oma's Ecke

Gulasch is wonderful served with potato dumplings (Thüringer Klösse; page 187) or egg noodles (Spätzle; page 60) and red cabbage (Apfel-Rotkohl; page 184) on the side. This really does bring back such wonderful memories of my *mutti*'s cooking, and I am ever thankful for all that she taught me.

Acknowledgments

I'm always amazed and so thankful for the people God brings into my life.

First and foremost, to my hubby, Andy, the love of my life for almost fifty years—you've always encouraged, inspired and motivated me, especially with my dream of publishing a print cookbook. We've had delicious adventures traveling throughout Germany, right in our kitchen.

Much gratitude to Will Kiester, president and publisher of Page Street Publishing, and his amazing team, in particular Elizabeth Seigle, Marissa Giambelluca and Meg Baskis, for enabling me to put my dream to paper, and to Toni Zernick, for cooking and photographing all.

To my dear friend, Heidi Möllgaard, *danke* (thank you) for constantly inspiring me, proofreading my German and sharing your secret recipes. And thanks to all my virtual friends and the Kaffeeklatschers who've helped in my research about strange ingredients and regional quirks, quickly steering me in the right direction.

Family hugs to my grandchildren, my boys and their wives—Alana, Lydia, Liam, Andrew & Vicki, Mike & Sylvie and Eran & Catherine—you are the inspiration to pass on my German heritage in such a yummy way. It's always a pleasure to cook for and with you. I look forward to spending many, many hours together, savoring the fruits of our labors.

About the Author

Gerhild Fulson is the author of *Just like Oma's Christmas Baking*, *Oma's Oktoberfest* and *Quick Fix Soups*, among other e-cookbooks. Having honed her skills at her *mutti's* side, and with her *mutti's* handwritten cookbook as a guide, Gerhild is now the *mutti* at whose side others are learning.

Known as Oma Gerhild to her many followers online, she is the cofounder of Gottes Wort ministry and a website consultant. Wanting to pass on her rich German heritage to her family, Gerhild took on the challenge to turn traditional recipes into time-friendly ones using ingredients that could be sourced outside of Germany. She leaned on the tips gleaned from her *mutti's* notes and now passes on that knowledge through her blog (*www.justlikeoma.com*), e-cookbooks and, for the first time, in print.

Born in Germany but raised in Canada, Gerhild lives in the picturesque Niagara region with Andy (a.k.a. Pastor Wolle), her husband of almost fifty years. Gerhild has three married sons and three grandchildren, and cooking for and with them sparks her creativity in the kitchen.

Passing on the distinctive German cuisine for a new generation to savor, Gerhild's recipes have become staples for those who crave their *oma's* home cooking of yesteryear.

Index